COWBOY

Hereford cow and calf

Four quirts made of braided leather and rawhide

Canadian cowboy
wearing storm gear

Modern cowboy
on quarter horse

Hand-tooled
leather A-fork
saddle, made
in Nevada
in the 1940s

Selection of
pocket watches

Old-style saddlemaker's tools

Texas cowboy
of the 1880s

Brand mark from the French Camargue

 EYEWITNESS BOOKS

COWBOY

Old-style leather holster with Colt .45 revolver

Written by
DAVID H. MURDOCH

Photographed by
GEOFF BRIGHTLING

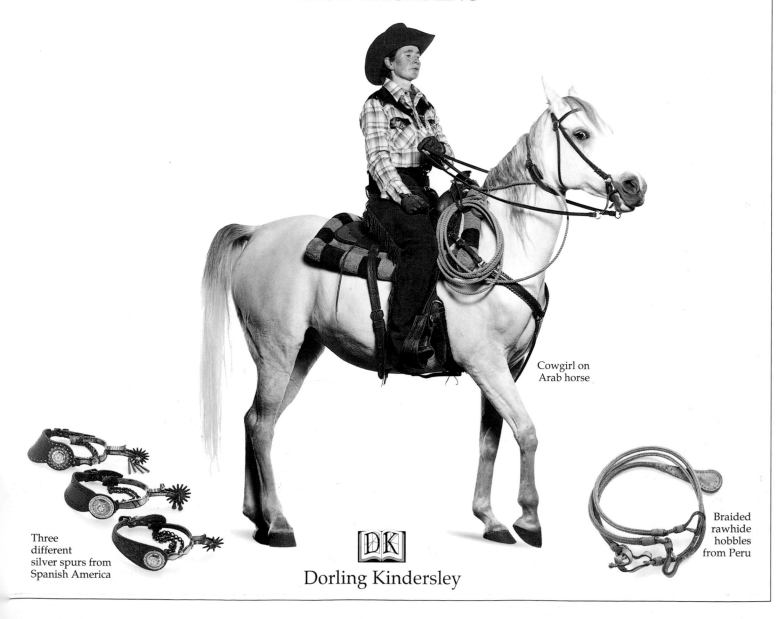

Cowgirl on Arab horse

Three different silver spurs from Spanish America

Braided rawhide hobbles from Peru

DK

Dorling Kindersley

Plains Indian rifle, 1870s

Replica of a U.S. lawman's badge

FEDERAL MARSHAL

Leather-covered metal water container, c. 1900

Modern Colombian stock saddle

South American gaucho

Cowboy wearing long johns

DK

Dorling Kindersley

LONDON, NEW YORK, AUCKLAND, DELHI, JOHANNESBURG, MUNICH, PARIS and SYDNEY

For a full catalog, visit

DK www.dk.com

Project editor Marion Dent
Art editor Jill Plank
Managing editor Helen Parker
Managing art editor Julia Harris
Researcher Céline Carez
Picture research Deborah Pownall
Production Catherine Semark
Additional photography Frank Greenaway
Editorial consultant Dr Paul Fees, Senior Curator, Buffalo Bill Historical Center, Cody, Wyoming

This Eyewitness ® Book has been conceived by Dorling Kindersley Limited and Editions Gallimard

© 1993 Dorling Kindersley Limited
This edition © 2000 Dorling Kindersley Limited
First American edition, 1993

Published in the United States by
DK Publishing, Inc.
375 Hudson Street,
New York, NY 10014
6 8 10 9 7 5

Dorling Kindersley books are available at special discounts for bulk purchases for sales promotions or premiums. Special editions, including personalized covers, excerpts of existing guides, and corporate imprints can be created in large quantities for specific needs. For more information, contact Special Markets Dept., Dorling Kindersley Publishing, Inc.

Library of Congress Cataloging-in-Publication Data
Murdoch, David Hamilton.
Cowboy / written by David H. Murdoch
p. cm.—(Eyewitness Books)
Includes index.
1. Cowboys—West (U.S.) 2. Cowboys.
I. Title. F596. M85 2000 978 — dc20   93-12768
ISBN 0-7894-5855-1 (pb)
ISBN 0-7894-5854-3 (hc)

Color reproduction by Colourscan, Singapore
Printed in China by Toppan Printing Co. (Shenzhen) Ltd.

Contents

6
What is a cowboy?
8
Charros and *vaqueros*
12
The best horses
14
Saddles – old and new
16
Saddling a horse
18
North American cowboy
20
Hats and more hats
22
Dressing a cowboy
24
Boots and spurs
26
Chaps in "chaps"
28
Life on a ranch
30
Cattle and branding
32
Cutting cattle out of a herd
36
Home on the range
38
On the trail drive
42
Law and order

44
Guns and gunslingers
46
Six gun
48
The South American gaucho
52
Camargue *Gardians*
56
Cowboys down under
58
Cowgirls
60
Cowboy culture
62
Rodeo thrills and spills
64
Index

Well-worn
American
cowboy boots,
1920s

What is a cowboy?

COWBOYS WERE FRONTIERSMEN. On the world's great grasslands, wherever cattle raising began and horses ran wild, cowboys lived and worked beyond the security of settlements and the comforts of civilization. The work, attracting men who were independent and self-reliant, required courage and endurance. Cowboys, therefore, believed that their work made them different from others and took pride in their lifestyle. Sometimes the authorities and city dwellers took another view; in the U.S. and Argentina, cowboys and gauchos were regarded as wild and dangerous. Yet in both countries they eventually came to symbolize values that the whole nation admired. This process has perhaps gone farthest in the U.S., where the cowboy has become the center of a myth built on the idea of the "Wild West." Hollywood has kept this myth alive, but the cowboys – and cowgirls – of western movies act out a fantasy that tells little of real life on the range.

THE COWBOYS OF SOUTH AMERICA
The horsemen who herded the cattle of the South American plains (pp. 48–51) had different names – gaucho in Argentina and Uruguay, *llanero* in Venezuela, and *huaso* in Chile – but shared a love of independence.

ITALIAN STYLE
The Romans called those who tended their herds of cattle *buteri*. The name has survived, for in modern times the cowboy of Italy is the *buttero*. He usually rides a particular breed of horse, the maremmana. Bred in Tuscany, in north central Italy, the maremmana is not very fast but is much prized for its endurance and calm, steady temperament.

CAMARGUE GARDIANS
In the salt marshes of the Rhône delta, in southern France, live the cowboys of the Camargue (pp. 52–55). Called *gardians*, for centuries they have bred special black bulls, raised solely for fighting. They still ride the unique white horses of the region. *Gardians* remain very proud of their traditions.

A *gardian* on his Camargue white horse

NORTH AFRICAN HORSEMEN
Members of the fierce warrior tribes of North Africa were superb horsemen. After their conversion to Islam, they began a war of conquest into Europe through Spain, but their relentless advance was finally stopped in France, in A.D. 732. They rode barb horses, famed for their endurance and remarkable speed over short distances. Barbs interbred with Spanish Andalusians (pp. 12–13), and so came to influence cowboy horses throughout the New World.

The powerful mustang – an ideal cow pony

6

THE FAMOUS NORTH AMERICAN COWBOY
North American cowboys (pp. 18–19) are the most famous in the world because of their imagined role in the Wild West. In reality, their work was hard, often monotonous, sometimes dangerous, and always badly paid. This, and the short heyday of the American cattle boom (1866–1887), meant that most were young. Many were Anglo-Americans, though the importance of Mexican, African, and Native Americans is often ignored. Perhaps no more than 35,000 cowboys actually drove cattle up the trails (pp. 38–41) or rode the range.

California A-fork style saddle, c. 1870

Silver concha

North American cowboy wearing batwing chaps

A HARD WORKING "HOSS"
Often the cowboy's mount was a mustang, a descendant of runaway Spanish Andalusians that had bred in the wild (pp. 12–13). Named from the Spanish *mesteña* for horse herd, the mustang was surefooted, tough, and fast. From 1900, wild mustangs were slaughtered for pet food until legally protected in 1970.

HUNGARY'S *CSIKOSOK*
The *puszta*, the great plain of Hungary, is home to the *csikosok*, the Hungarian cowboy. Famed for their skills as horsemen, *csikoski* are herders of both horses and the region's gray, long-horned cattle. Their dress (blue for horse herders, white for cattlemen) is traditional, as is the use of long whips.

CHARROS* AND *VAQUEROS
New World cattle ranching began in Mexico, the first part of the continent to be colonized by the Spaniards in the early 1500s. Land-owning *charros* and their working cowboys (pp. 8–11), the *vaqueros*, developed the skills later taken over by American cowboys. Their influence is shown by the many Spanish terms in the cowboys' work vocabulary.

Charros and vaqueros

THE SPANISH SETTLERS OF MEXICO in the early 1500s brought long-horned Iberian cattle and Andalusian horses to a continent that previously had no horses or cattle. Many colonists turned to cattle ranching, a profitable as well as "honorable" occupation, because of the great demand for hides, horn, meat, and tallow. By 1848, when Mexico lost much territory to the U.S., ranching had spread to Texas and California. Rich, ranch-owning *charros* liked to display their wealth with personal ornaments of silver, much of it from the great mines at Zacatecas in north central Mexico. Ranching techniques spread from Mexico throughout the Americas, and horses that escaped into the wild became the mustangs of the U.S., the pasos of Peru, and the criollos of Argentina.

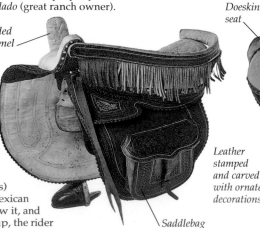

A MAGNIFICENT MOUNT
Charros sometimes imported horses from the U.S., like this palomino saddlebred, a strong breed from Kentucky, capable of covering great distances without tiring. Long, wedge-shaped, leather covers on the stirrups, called *tapaderos*, prevented the rider's feet from slipping through the stirrups, being ripped by thorny brush – or bitten by the horse!

Rawhide-edged, leather holster, holding an expensive version of a model 1872 Colt .45, with silver butt plate and gold strap

Classic-style tapaderos *are long and slim*

Back view of *charro* on horseback

Elaborately decorated with fantastical animals and serpents

Shape of broad-armed cross

CRUCIFORM STIRRUPS
Stirrups, used in Europe from the eighth century, were essential for heavily armed riders to stay in the saddle, but lightly armed Asian nomads and Native Americans fought without them. These iron stirrups may have belonged to a 16th-century Spanish conquistador, or conqueror, in Mexico. Elaborately decorated, their shape echoed their rider's role as a Christian soldier of the cross.

SILVER SADDLE
This magnificent *charro* saddle was made about 1870 by David Lozano, *talabartería* (saddlemaker) of Mexico City. The artistic tooling, stitching in silver-covered thread, silver-plated conchas (decorative disks), and solid silver on the saddle horn and behind the cantle, all suggest that this was the property of a *hacendado* (great ranch owner).

Horn shaped like an upturned horse's hoof

Solid silver decoration on cantle

Silver monogram on stirrup

Heavily tooled leather showing village scenes and floral designs

Silver concha

A FINE SEAT
From the 1600s, women (condemned to wear long, heavy skirts) were able to ride only by using a sidesaddle. This late 1800s Mexican sidesaddle has a support rail on the left, with a saddlebag below it, and a shoe stirrup on the right side. With her right foot in the stirrup, the rider crooked her left knee around the padded pommel, resting her left foot on her right knee – this is much more secure than it looks! The doeskin seat and elaborate decoration show how wealthy the owner was.

Padded pommel

Doeskin seat

Saddle rail

Leather stamped and carved with ornate decorations

Saddlebag

View of left side

View of right side

Built-in shoe stirrup

Ladies' sidesaddle, Mexican, late 1800s

Wide-brimmed, black felt
sombrero to keep sun off

Fine quality,
brown suede
jacket and
trousers

Finely woven
cotton scarf

Double-ear style
bridle lavishly
decorated with
silver to match
the saddle

Heavy cotton shirt
with embroidered
panels on front

TRUE CRAFTMANSHIP
British craftsmen were aware of the worldwide
growth of ranching in the 1800s. This illustration –
of an all-purpose Spanish-American cowboy – is
from *The Saddles of all Nations*, a book published by
Thomas Newton to advertise his products. Newton,
who died in 1889, took over his father's lorimer
business (maker of bits, spurs, and stirrups) when
he was 17 and then became the first saddlemaker
in Walsall, which is near Birmingham in England.

Double-skinned
leather makes saddle
much stronger and
much more
expensive

Hand-tooled leather
saddle weighs 55 lb
(25 kg) and has
elaborate silver
decoration on horn,
A-fork, and gullet

Hand-engraved
silver conchas
on matching
breast harness

Black and white
"corona," or
saddle blanket

CHAMPION CHARRO
The dress and riding gear of the *charro* were both practical
and a visible sign of his status. He inherited his superb
horsemanship from his Spanish ancestors who accompanied
early explorers, like Hernando Cortés (1485–1547), to Mexico.
The men who worked on the great *haciendas*, or ranches, owned
by the wealthy *charros*, were the poor *vaqueros*. A *vaquero*
owned no land, probably not even a horse, but he began the
noble tradition of the itinerant working cowboy that spread
from Mexico into the U.S. and Canada (pp. 18–19).

Mexican *charro*
on a ten-year-old
palomino American
saddlebred – with
matching bridle,
breast harness, and
saddle made by the
Swedish-American
Edward H. Bohlin
(1895–1980),
"saddlemaker to the
stars" of Hollywood
westerns (pp. 60–61).

Continued on next page

Continued from previous page

Silver horseshoe

Silver thread-
work in
leather

A SUPERLATIVE SADDLE
This *charro* saddle (late 1800s) is finely
ornamented with a silver horn, elegant bow
design, and silver threads worked into the
leather. The hand-tooling served a practical
purpose – the friction it created helped
the rider stay in the saddle.

Embossed silver
rim on cantle

The valiant *vaqueros*

Vaqueros (from the Spanish *vaca* for cow), though
from Mexico's peasantry, felt they were superior
to farmers. They were proud of their work, which
they believed demanded courage, fortitude, and
physical endurance. Like gauchos (pp. 48–51),
they scorned firearms for settling personal
quarrels. In 1823, Hawaii's King Kamehameha III
sent for *vaqueros* to train his men as *paniola* (cowboys). In California, New Mexico, and Texas,
Mexican-American *vaqueros* formed an important proportion of ranch hands in the late 1800s.

Very fine Mexican
saddle (late 1800s)
with matching
cinch (below)
and spur (right)

SUNDAY-BEST CLOTHES
Formal, "Sunday-best"
clothes were worn for
attending church,
marriages and funerals,
and for fiestas. Though
reflecting the climate
and traditions of Mexico,
they show something of
their origins in 17th- and
18th-century Spain.

Silver bow design
of cinch's buckle is
repeated on both
saddle and spur

Jinglebob spur, c. 1900, made by G. S. Garcia (1864–1933), a bit, spur, and saddlemaker expert in the California style of elaborate inlaid design

Hand-tooled leather

Hand-engraved silver concha

Half-moon shape denotes Islamic origins

Mexican inlaid silver spur, c. 1890

A FINE SENSE OF STYLE
Mexican spurs often show the owner's sense of style and love of finery – these half-drop shank spurs are inlaid with silver. Attached to the rowel pins are tiny jinglebobs that tinkle with every movement. This spur with its three silver studs shows an Islamic influence where even numbers are perfect – and unlucky!

Silver stud

Jinglebob

FROM BUFFALO BILL'S WILD WEST SHOW
Also inlaid with silver, these straight-shank spurs were once worn by a member of Buffalo Bill's Wild West show.

A *vaquero* on a criollo

A WORKING VAQUERO
Vaqueros' working clothes varied. Some wore a plain short jacket, flared woolen trousers, and a felt sombrero (pp. 20–21). Poorer men dressed more like peasants (*peóns*), with a cloak (*serape*), cotton pants, and a straw hat.

A RICH OWNER
Such lavish and careful attention to detail suggest this spur (as well as the saddle and cinch) was the property of a man of wealth – and some vanity.

LIKE A ROOSTER'S FOOT
Prick spurs, shaped like the spur claw of a fighting cock, were less common than rowel spurs.

Mexican prick spur showing its Moorish influence

Spur measures 5.5 in (14 cm) long

"Niello" inlay, made by silver wire hammered into the steel

An 8-point, straight-shank rowel spur

ASSORTED QUIRTS
Mexican quirts (from the Spanish *cuerta* for whip) were made from braided rawhide. The wooden grip could be filled with lead shot in order to beat down a rearing horse or restrain an untamed one when breaking it.

Mexican quirt, c. 1900

Latigo leather thong

Braided rawhide

BUFFALO BILL'S WILD WEST

ROUGH RIDERS OF THE WORLD
William "Buffalo Bill" Cody (1846–1917) – buffalo hunter, scout, actor, dime novel hero – formed the first Wild West show in 1883 (pp. 60–61) and toured the U.S. and Europe for over 30 years. One act, "Rough Riders of the World," featured many kinds of horsemen, including *vaqueros* (left above).

IT'S A CINCH
This cinch (from the Spanish *cincha* for saddle girth) matches the saddle and spur (far left and above). It is made from fine cream cotton cord, and the dangling pieces are "shoo flies" – which are meant to do exactly what the name suggests.

Cinch made of fine cream cotton cord

Blue and cream shoo fly made of fine wool

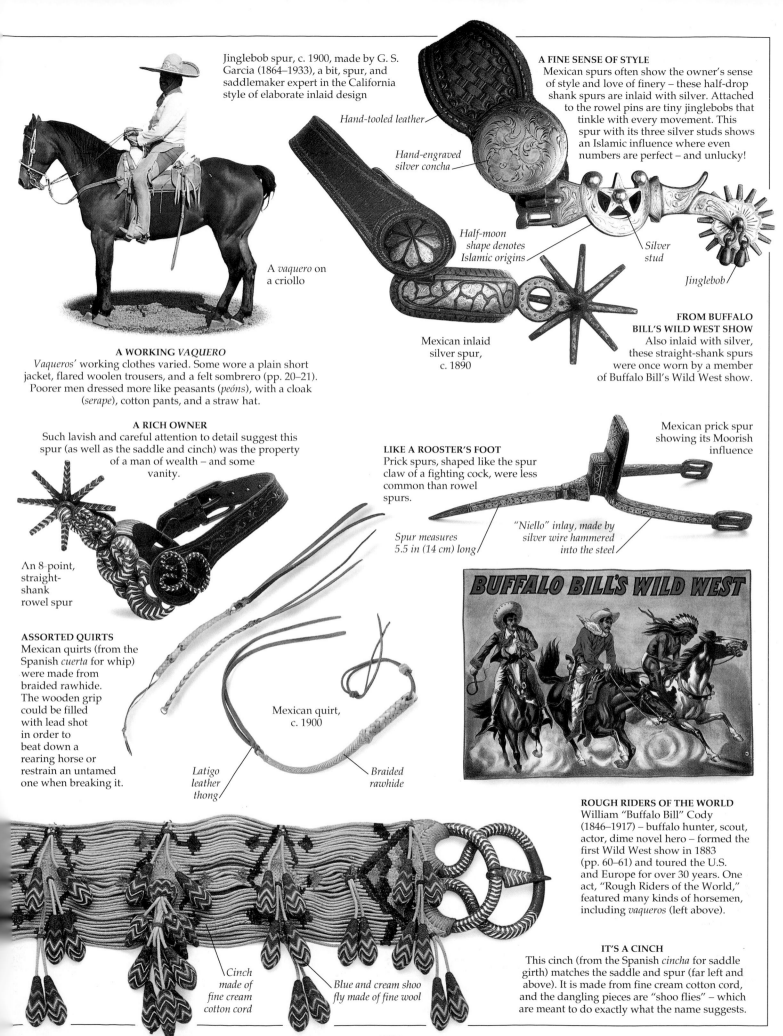

The best horses

HORSES AND PEOPLE HAVE WORKED TOGETHER since wild horses were first domesticated, probably in eastern Europe 4,000 years ago. Horses changed the direction of human history. They enabled nomadic cultures to range across continents. As chariot pullers and then cavalry mounts, horses transformed warfare. They became the tractors of premodern agriculture and were essential to any kind of large-scale cattle raising. Wild horses died out, except for the Przewalski. All present-day horses are descended from these original, domesticated animals and form one species – *Equus caballus*. Cross-breeding and different environments have created different colors, sizes, abilities, and characteristics.

Built-in saddlebag

"TURN HIM LOOSE, BILL"
This painting by Frederic Remington (pp. 26–27) shows a cowboy "breaking" an untamed horse. After getting the horse used to a hackamore, or training bridle, and saddle, cowboys tried to ride the bucking animal to a standstill, in order to break its resistance. The cruel use of quirt and spurs was common.

EASTERN COWBOY
The conquering horde of Genghis Khan (1162?–1227), which created an empire from China west to the Black Sea, rode shaggy Mongol ponies. Kazakh herdsmen in northwest China still ride these animals' descendants.

Flank cinch is loose, so that slack is taken up when roped calf pulls on lariat attached to saddle horn

A TEXAS COW PONY
This Texas cowboy, c. 1885, is riding a mustang. Both Native Americans and cowboys used mustangs, descendants of 15th-century Andalusians that had escaped and multiplied across the North American plains. Though small, the cow pony had great endurance and was hard working.

THE GAUCHOS' COW PONY
Like the mustang of the north, the criollo is descended from feral Andalusians (pp. 8–9) that wandered into South America from Mexico. Strong, agile, and surefooted, in Argentina it became the cow pony of the gauchos (pp. 48–51) – the cowboys of the pampas. Crossed with thoroughbreds, criollos produced the famous Argentinian polo ponies.

THE FIRST AMERICAN BREED
Settlers in 17th-century Virginia crossed their English horses with Spanish (Andalusian) stock to produce the quarter horse – the first American breed. Named for the popular colonial sport of quarter-mile races, the quarter horse could produce an extraordinary burst of speed. This, combined with its balance, agility, and great strength, made the breed an ideal cow pony.

Horn secures lariat once a wild horse or calf has been lassoed

Headstall made of braided rawhide

Breast collar

"Joe's Fancy Freckle," a 6-year-old female quarter horse, 14.3 hands high – a hand measures 4 in (10.16 cm) at the withers

CREAM OF THE CAMARGUE
Perhaps descended from the Asian mounts of the Huns who invaded Europe in A.D. 300–400, these white horses breed wild in the marshes of the Camargue (pp. 52–55) in southern France.

Camargue of France

A "HUNGARY" HORSE
Descended from a 19th-century Norman (French) stallion, the Hungarian nonius was developed by mating offspring with several other breeds. Though not fast, it is a tough, reliable, all-purpose animal.

Nonius of Hungary

ANCIENT ANDALUSIAN
A very old breed from the south of Spain, the Andalusian was taken by the conquistadors to the New World in the early 1600s. Its great qualities are strength and endurance.

Andalusian of Spain

PORTUGUESE PONY
Similar to the Andalusian, the lusitano of Portugal was once prized as a cavalry horse. Its courage and agility make it the ideal choice for the bullfighters of Portugal.

BELL FOR A "BELL MARE"
Just as bells are still put around the necks of lead bulls or cows in the French Camargue (pp. 52–55), bells used to be put on bell, or lead, mares in North America. The bell helped to locate a herd of grazing horses and keep them from wandering away.

Lusitano of Portugal

COSSACK WARRIORS
The Cossack warrior tribes of Russia were outstanding horsemen who made formidable light cavalry, first as enemies of the expanding Czarist Empire, then from the 1800s as part of the Imperial Army. Their Don horses, bred on the Russian steppes, were amazingly hardy, able to survive on the poorest food.

Saddles – old and new

A COWBOY SAT ON HIS HORSE for up to 15 hours a day – he did not sit behind a steering wheel or at an office desk. His saddle was, therefore, his most important piece of equipment. Unlike his horse (pp. 12–13), which probably was one of several loaned to him by the rancher, his saddle was his own and cost at least a month's wages – but it would last 30 years. Cowboy saddles evolved from the 16th-century Spanish war saddle, with its high pommel (combination of horn and fork at the front) and cantle (the raised part of the seat at the back) to hold its armored rider in place. Over time they changed in weight and shape, but all were built on a wooden frame (pp. 16–17) covered with wet rawhide – which made the frame rigid as it dried – then re-covered with dressed leather.

DEEP IN THE HEART OF TEXAS
This 1850s Texas saddle had a thick horn for heavy roping and fenders to keep horse sweat off the rider's legs.

A-fork frame

Short skirt

AN A-FORK
This 1870s California saddle has an A-fork frame (from its shape), a slim horn, and steam-bent wooden stirrups. Lighter than Texas or Denver saddles, it burdened the horse less.

HIGH POINT
The Denver saddle (c. 1890) was longer than the one from Texas (top), with more leather covering. Cowboys liked the solid seat it gave, but its length and weight (40 lb, or 18 kg) sometimes gave the horses back sores.

Cantle at back of saddle

FROM OLD MEXICO
This battered Mexican saddle shows the link with 16th-century warriors' saddles. The horn and cantle are carved wood, and the simple frame is covered with tooled leather.

Carved wooden horn at front of saddle

Mexican saddle, made of leather and wood

CUTTING SADDLE
This 1890s Canadian stock saddle – for cutting out and rope work – is double-cinched. The flank (rear) cinch is kept loose, so the strain on the saddle horn from a roped cow will pull the saddle forward and signal the horse to stop (pp. 34–35).

Front cinch

Flank strap, or cinch

Hooded 1920s taps made from very strong cowhide leather

Stamped cowhide 1970s taps with sheepskin lining for extra warmth

ONE FROM THE NORTH
After the 1870s, saddles from the northern ranges of Montana and Wyoming had leather over the horn and usually square skirts.

Pommel

Cantle

TOUGH TAPS
Taps (from the Spanish *tapaderos*, pp. 8–11) fitted over the stirrup and gave the rider's foot extra protection from thornbrush and from rain and snow in winter. The two pairs above were called "hawg's snout" from their pig-nose shape; the pair on the right is in the "eagle's beak" style.

Taps (1890s) from Buffalo Bill's Wild West show

CAMARGUE STYLE
A Camargue *gardian's* saddle (pp. 52–55) has a curved cantle, a broad, solid pommel, and metal, cage-shaped stirrups. Below the pommel, always on the left, is tied his *seden* (rope).

Horn

A-fork frame – at front of saddle

Engraved silver over saddle's gullet

Seat

Silver-covered cantle at back of saddle

Rear jockey

Wool saddle pad

Square skirt

Large silver concha

SILVERED SADDLE
This splendid saddle was made by Edward H. Bohlin (pp. 8–9). The cantle and horn decorations are silver, as are the A-fork frame at the front of the saddle, and the conchas around the skirts, fenders, and on the taps. All the covering leather is hand-tooled. The total weight is 55 lb (25 kg).

Ornate, heavily tooled leather

Cord cinch goes around horse's middle to hold saddle secure

Wrapped horn prevents wear and tear when roping

CENTER-FIRE RIG
Center-fire rigs, like this 1980s California stock saddle, have a single, central cinch, giving good balance and ability to take average roping strain.

Braided rawhide quirt

Eagle's beak taps

Fender

Leather tie for attaching extra items to saddle

Rope, made from "maguey" (century plant), tied to saddle horn

Silver monogram

American-made 1970s saddle

Low cantle

RODEO STYLE
No horn is needed on this modern 1950s Australian rodeo saddle – and the skirts are minimized.

Metal studs on skirt for harder wear

RIMFIRE
This 1970s stock saddle uses the Spanish "rimfire" rig with a cinch around the front of the horse's stomach and a flank strap.

Connecting strap

DOUBLE-RIGGED
Double-rigged saddles need a flank strap to keep it from tipping up at the back when roping. A connecting strap to the cinch keeps the flank strap from slipping back.

15

Saddling a horse

SITTING SECURELY ON AN ANIMAL over 5 ft (1.6 m) high, and being able to control it, the cowboy was the inheritor of age-old knowledge of the horse. Bridles were used by the Egyptians by 1600 B.C., although horse riders sat on pads or cloths until the saddle was invented around A.D. 350. Stirrups were first used by the Huns a century later. In the 16th century, Spanish cavalry were the finest and best equipped in Europe, and Spaniards took their skills with them to the Americas. American cowboys later took this knowledge and adapted it. The cowboy's saddle (pp. 14–15) was a work platform on which he also had to carry his equipment. The bridle was designed to check the horse with the slightest pull on the reins.

Split-ear bridle

1 ON WITH THE BRIDLE
Without a bridle, a horse cannot be controlled, so the bridle is put on first. It is made up of a bit and a headstall (split to go around the horse's ears) to hold it in place. The bit is a metal bar resting forward in the horse's mouth, so that the horse cannot get the bit between his teeth and bolt!

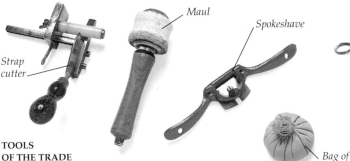

Strap cutter

Maul

Spokeshave

Raised plate

Slobber chain

Half moon

A MARMALUKE BIT
Like the old-style Spanish-American spade bit, the marmaluke bit had a raised plate that lay across the horse's tongue. Only the gentlest touch was used on the reins, so as not to cause the horse pain. Reins were attached to "slobber chains," so the horse did not soak the leather.

TOOLS OF THE TRADE
Saddlemaker's tools are simple. The strap cutter adjusts for cutting different widths of leather. The heavy maul, or hammer, is padded to prevent damage to the leather. Like the carpenter's tool, the spokeshave planes curves. The bag of shot holds down the leather without marking it, while the crescent knife allows a firm grip when cutting out curves in leather.

Bag of shot

Crescent knife

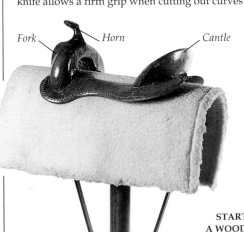

Fork *Horn* *Cantle*

Leather skirt

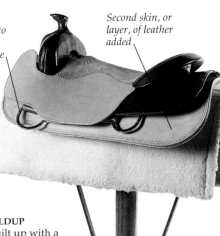

Rigging ring to attach front cinch to saddle

Second skin, or layer, of leather added

START WITH A WOODEN TREE
Made from straight-grained, knot-free pine, the tree contains the metal horn screwed to the fork. This is then covered in wet rawhide, which is dried at a controlled temperature, then given several coats of water-proof lacquer.

Basic wooden tree with several coats of lacquer

THE BUILDUP
The saddle is built up with a series of coverings beginning with the horn, then the underside of the fork, the seat, fork, cantle, and skirts. Different thicknesses of leather are used, each shaped, then stitched with damp rawhide.

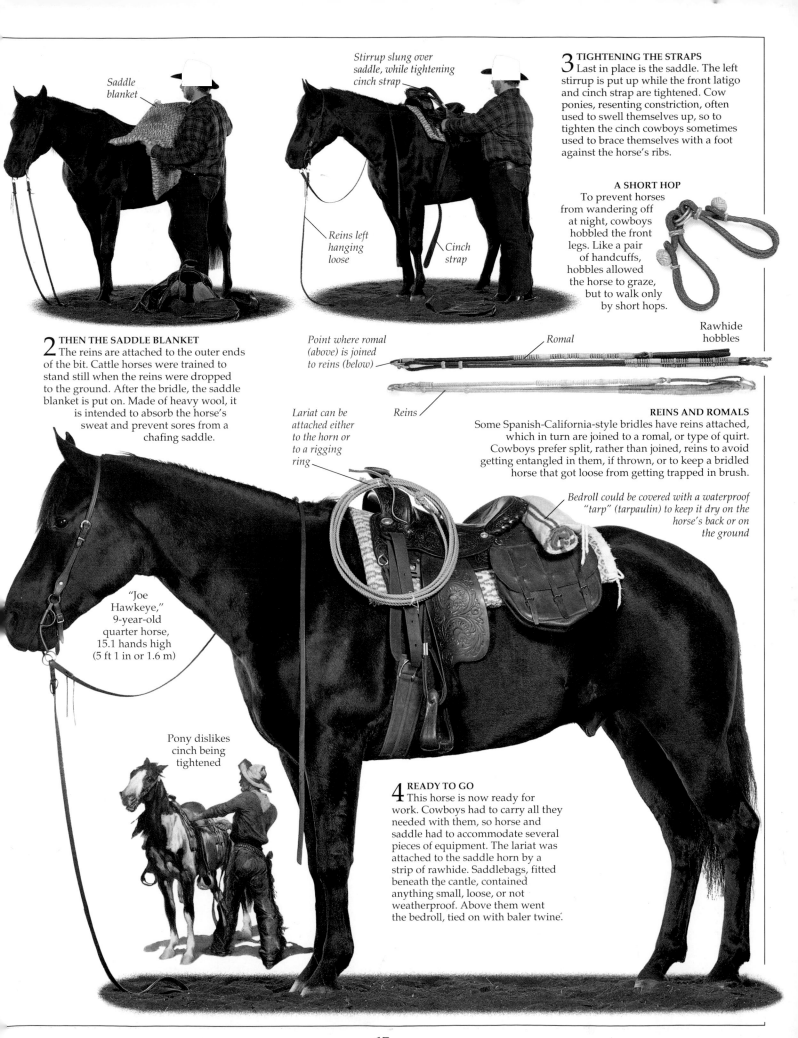

Saddle
blanket

Stirrup slung over
saddle, while tightening
cinch strap

3 TIGHTENING THE STRAPS
Last in place is the saddle. The left
stirrup is put up while the front latigo
and cinch strap are tightened. Cow
ponies, resenting constriction, often
used to swell themselves up, so to
tighten the cinch cowboys sometimes
used to brace themselves with a foot
against the horse's ribs.

Reins left
hanging
loose

Cinch
strap

A SHORT HOP
To prevent horses
from wandering off
at night, cowboys
hobbled the front
legs. Like a pair
of handcuffs,
hobbles allowed
the horse to graze,
but to walk only
by short hops.

Rawhide
hobbles

2 THEN THE SADDLE BLANKET
The reins are attached to the outer ends
of the bit. Cattle horses were trained to
stand still when the reins were dropped
to the ground. After the bridle, the saddle
blanket is put on. Made of heavy wool, it
is intended to absorb the horse's
sweat and prevent sores from a
chafing saddle.

Point where romal
(above) is joined
to reins (below)

Romal

Reins

REINS AND ROMALS
Some Spanish-California-style bridles have reins attached,
which in turn are joined to a romal, or type of quirt.
Cowboys prefer split, rather than joined, reins to avoid
getting entangled in them, if thrown, or to keep a bridled
horse that got loose from getting trapped in brush.

Lariat can be
attached either
to the horn or
to a rigging
ring

Bedroll could be covered with a waterproof
"tarp" (tarpaulin) to keep it dry on the
horse's back or on
the ground

"Joe
Hawkeye,"
9-year-old
quarter horse,
15.1 hands high
(5 ft 1 in or 1.6 m)

Pony dislikes
cinch being
tightened

4 READY TO GO
This horse is now ready for
work. Cowboys had to carry all they
needed with them, so horse and
saddle had to accommodate several
pieces of equipment. The lariat was
attached to the saddle horn by a
strip of rawhide. Saddlebags, fitted
beneath the cantle, contained
anything small, loose, or not
weatherproof. Above them went
the bedroll, tied on with baler twine.

North American cowboys

COWBOYS' WORK was hard and badly paid. Most American cowboys came from the South, others from the East and Midwest, and Europe (after foreign investment in the 1880s). Their heyday began with the Texas trail drives in 1866 and ended 20 years later when open-range ranching collapsed due to falling prices, farmers fencing in land, and the terrible winter of 1886–1887. In Canada, cowboys worked on the big ranches that sprang up in the 1880s, but there, too, farmers, and finally the bad winter of 1907, ended the old way of life. The cowboy became merely an employee in a new, reorganized business. Up to 1885, cowboys were unjustly despised in American newspapers as wild, drunken ruffians – then their disappearing way of life was seen as romantic, and the cowboy became a national hero. Writers and artists began nostalgically to praise the cowboy's courage, self-reliance, and individualism – qualities that seemed to have been lost in an industrial America.

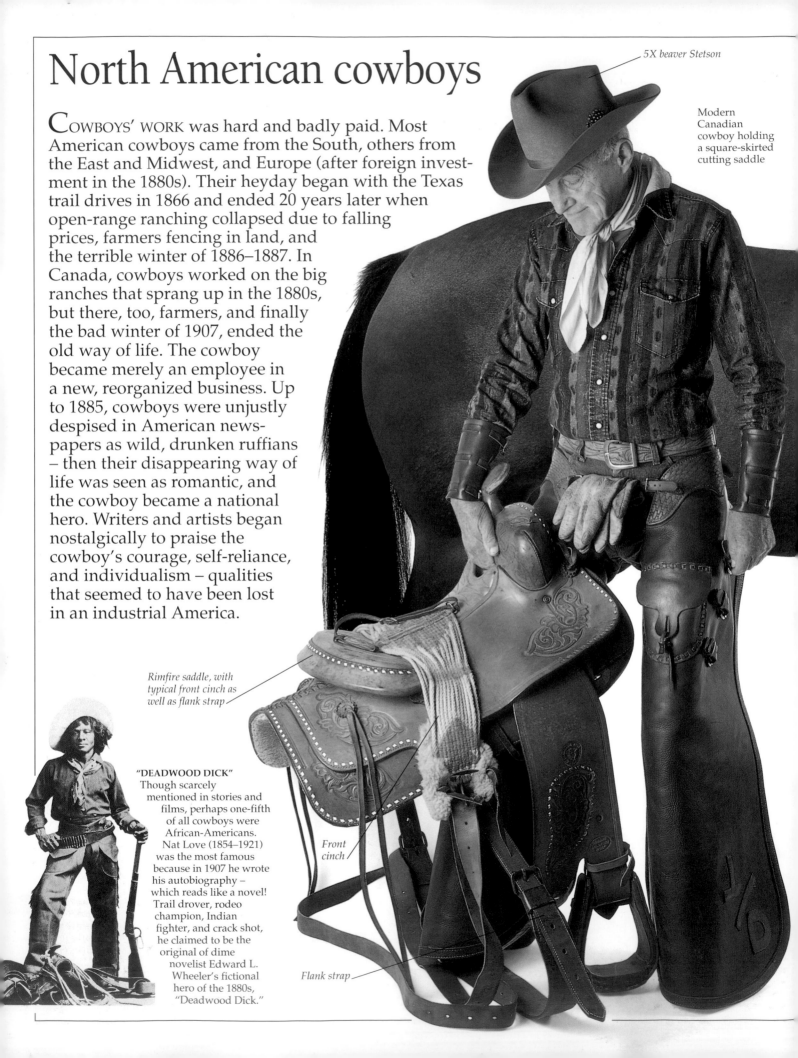

5X beaver Stetson

Modern Canadian cowboy holding a square-skirted cutting saddle

Rimfire saddle, with typical front cinch as well as flank strap

"DEADWOOD DICK"
Though scarcely mentioned in stories and films, perhaps one-fifth of all cowboys were African-Americans. Nat Love (1854–1921) was the most famous because in 1907 he wrote his autobiography – which reads like a novel! Trail drover, rodeo champion, Indian fighter, and crack shot, he claimed to be the original of dime novelist Edward L. Wheeler's fictional hero of the 1880s, "Deadwood Dick."

Front cinch

Flank strap

COWBOYS IN A MODERN WORLD

Modern cowboys work in a modern industry. Ranches have declined in size and number since 1940 and most employ 75 percent fewer hands. Cowboys and horses are now ferried from ranch to pasture by truck and trailer, and in rough country some ranchers use helicopters for herding. Growth of mechanized branding has reduced the need for roping, while the use of pickup trucks has created "windshield cowboys." Nevertheless, the old skills are still valuable, particularly at roundup time and in horse breaking (now done with much more care). Cowboys still ride quarter horses (though with better saddles), and their dress has hardly changed at all.

MONTANA BOUND

After an 1881 trip to Montana, New York artist Frederic Remington was determined to record the dying Old West. So, too, was future president Theodore Roosevelt (1858–1919), who in 1888 wrote *Ranch Life and the Hunting Trail*, which shows this illustration by Remington.

A Montana cowboy wearing Angora goat chaps, or "woolies," and carrying a quirt

Quarter horse

A pinto, with "ovaro" markings

A spotted appaloosa

SPOT THE DIFFERENCE

Some cowboys and many Native Americans preferred horses with distinctive coloring, like pintos and appaloosas. The pinto (paint) is either brown with white splashes (ovaro) or white with brown splashes (tobiano). The strikingly spotted appaloosa is named after the Palouse River in Oregon, where they were first bred in the 1700s by the Nez Percé tribe.

NATIVE AMERICAN STYLE

Looking back, some ranchers later admitted that the best cowboys were Indians! In Oklahoma (former Indian Territory), many cowboys were recruited from the Native American tribes who had been forced to settle there. They dressed like Anglo cowboys, but kept ethnic touches like the feather and beading on this hat – made by an English company that exported to the West.

AN OLD COWHAND – FROM ARIZONA

By 1901, when he painted this portrait of an old-time Arizona cowboy, Remington was relying on his memory, notes, and models. The details are accurate, but the artist was deliberately creating an exciting image to suit public demand for a romantic West.

FLYING THE FLAG

The birthplace of American ranching, Texas has always been somehow the "real" Wild West. Originally part of Mexico, Texas was settled by Americans who rebelled in 1836. After the heroic, but hopeless defense of the Alamo, Texans defeated the Mexican armies, and Texas became an independent republic, until it joined the U.S. in 1845.

Hats and more hats

A COWBOY'S HAT was his trademark. Styles might vary – from sombreros to Stetsons – but the functions were the same. In blazing sun, the high crown kept the head cool while the broad brim shaded the eyes and neck. In rain and snow the hat was a mini-umbrella; it also protected against thorns and low-hanging branches. Made of high quality felt, it was meant to take years of wear. This was fortunate because a cowboy used his versatile hat as an alternative to a quirt (pp. 10–11), to carry water (as shown in the famous Stetson label), to fan fires (or put them out), and occasionally even as a pillow.

Australian akubra

Gardian's hat

TWO HATS
Because they meet the same needs, cowboys' hats around the world look remarkably similar. The distinctive Australian akubra is worn all over the outback and particularly by stockmen (pp. 56–57). The modern *gardian's* hat (pp. 52–55) is from the French Camargue.

the last drop from his STETSON

FAMOUS LABEL
After 1885, Stetson hats (with the famous label) were worn by most westerners. By 1906, the company was selling two million per year.

FILM STAR'S HAT
Roy Rogers strengthened the "good guy" tradition by always wearing a white hat.

Braided decoration embroidered with gold wire meant its owner was wealthy

MEXICAN HAT DANCE
This elegant pre-1870s Mexican felt hat is decorated with gold wire embroidery. Its very broad brim, braided-horsehair band and tall crown (called a "sugarloaf" because of its shape) make it a sombrero (from the Spanish *sombra* for shade).

A SOU'WESTER?
The low-crown plainsman's hat with a floppy brim was an alternative to the sombrero in Mexico. It was widely worn by cowboys in the southwestern U.S. up to the 1880s.

Hatband made of rope

Hatband made
from broken
braided rein

"TWENTY-GALLON TENDERFOOT"
In *Son of Paleface*, Bob Hope (b. 1903) wears a double ten-gallon hat as a "tenderfoot" pretending to be a westerner.

Wide-brimmed black Stetson, c. 1900

5X beaver Tom Mix-style Stetson

A FAMILY OF HATTERS
Englishman John B. Stetson (1830–1906) learned about Westerners' needs while gold prospecting in Colorado. From a family of hatters, he opened a factory in Philadelphia, Pennsylvania, in 1865 and soon produced the design that became famous – and made him a multimillionaire.

TOP HAT
A high-crowned hat was nicknamed the "ten-gallon" hat. This double ten-gallon hat should earn its wearer some stares!

FILM STAR
In 1925, the Stetson company named a hat for cowboy film star Tom Mix (pp. 60–61). It had a 7.5-in (19.5-cm) crown and 5-in (13-cm) brim.

Stiff brim

MODERN STETSON
Today's Stetsons meet the modern preference for a lower crown. This one is top quality and water-resistant, creased in the cattleman's style. The number next to the "X" denotes the quality of the hat's material – the higher the number, the better the quality.

Best quality 10X beaver Stetson

Horsehair tassel

HOOKED ON HATS
In the Old West, it was not considered impolite to wear one's hat in the house. However, if provided, a hatstand also made good use of horns and hide.

A HANDSOME HAT
Stetsons never had any decoration, except for a fancy hatband, perhaps. Mexican sombreros, however, were often ornamented – this one has suede appliqué and leather tassels.

Brim bound with leather

NOT SO PLAIN PLAINSMAN
The plainsman's style came in more expensive versions, such as this Mexican hat, c. 1900, made of suede with appliqué ribbon trim.

WEAR AND TEAR!
This Mexican hat has seen some hard wear. Dating from the early 1900s, it was probably the working headgear of a *vaquero*. It also looks like those that Hollywood always insisted bandits wear in silent westerns!

STRAW SOMBRERO
Less durable, but less expensive than felt hats, Mexican sombreros were sometimes made of straw – like this one, c. 1900.

LUCKY LUKE
The invention of French cartoonist "Morris" (Maurice de Bevère), Lucky Luke has been cheerfully cleaning up the West since 1946. He still rides Jolly Jumper and hums "I'm a poor lonesome cowboy. . ."

Dressing a cowboy

A COWBOY WOULD CHOOSE HIS CLOTHES and equipment to cope with the often brutally hard work, the country, and the climate. Clothing had to be strong to withstand heavy wear-and-tear from working closely with animals amid thorny brush. It had to deal with both scorching hot days and freezing cold nights. Differences in local conditions and local customs created different styles of cowboy dress in the U.S. between the southwest, such as New Mexico and Texas, and the northern ranges of Wyoming, Montana, and the Dakotas. Revolvers were supposedly necessary to deal with threats both animal and human, but some cowboys could not afford them – a new Colt could cost a month's wages. Northern ranchers tried to discourage their cowhands from carrying guns. Cowboys also followed fashion – one old ranch hand confessed that high-heeled boots were worn out of vanity, not necessity!

Colt .45 in a leather holster

HIGH-RIDER HOLSTER
Common through the 1870s and 1880s was the "high-rider" holster, which was fitted over the belt, so that the gun rested high on the hip. The cutaway for the trigger guard, as well as practice, helped a fast draw.

Convenience flap

Long johns were usually made of red wool

1 STARTING THE DAY
Day began with coffee, made from beans probably crushed between two rocks; it was drunk black, without sugar. At work, cowboys rarely took off their one-piece "long johns" – the convenience flap at the back removed the only necessity to do so! Usually made of red wool, long johns provided insulation during cold nights. Of more importance, in the heat of the day, they absorbed sweat that otherwise would quickly rot a shirt.

Silver-plated railroad watch

ON TIME
Pocket watches were more ornamental than useful – cowboys would keep them in their bedroll rather than risk breaking or losing them while working. A "one-dollar railroad watch" (top) was usually a retirement present to a railroad worker, but was also sold in town stores. Gold- and silver-plated watches (below) could be bought from Montgomery Ward or Sears & Roebuck mail order catalogs (pp. 28–29) and carried 20-year guarantees.

Plain, gold-plated watch

Silver-plated with floral engraving

Lace and buckle fastenings

Early 1900s cuffs from California

Four sets of cuffs, showing both decorations and fastenings

ALL SORTS OF CUFFS
When using their lariat, cowboys usually wore gloves, made of buck-skin, to avoid rope burns. From the early 1900s, they also wore stiff leather cuffs, from 5–7 in (13–18 cm) long, sometimes with a strap or laces to tighten them. Cuffs both protected the wrists and also trapped loose shirt sleeves. Saddlers catered to cowboy vanity by stamping various designs into the leather.

Snap and lace fastenings

Stamped leather decoration

Basket-stamped leather

2 THE NEXT STEP
Shirt and pants were made of long-wearing, heavy wool, but tightly buckled leather belts risked internal injury to a rider on a bucking horse. So this cowboy is wearing a pair of ex-cavalry suspenders, though many cowboys did not like such "galluses."

3 ALL SET TO GO
Ready for work, the cowboy has knotted his cotton bandana, which protects his neck from the sun and acts as a mask against dust. He is also wearing a Mexican-style waistcoat. High-top work boots, with sloped 2-in (5-cm) heels and rowel spurs, stovepipe chaps, and a high-crowned Stetson complete his outfit.

Sterling silver belt buckles from California

COWBOY JEWELRY
Generally, a belt buckle was the only decoration a cowboy would wear. Buckles did not become popular until the 1920s, when they were given out as prizes in rodeos (pp. 62–63). They were often made of precious metals, such as gold and sterling silver, and even included jewels like rubies or diamonds.

Modern copy of old-style, high-crowned Stetson

Heavy wool shirt

Cotton print bandana

Ex-military suspenders

Hatband made of braided leather reins

Saddle blanket

Striped, Mexican-style waistcoat

Pin-striped wool trousers

Old-style, high-rider holster made of basket-weave leather

Fringed leather shotgun chaps with front pockets

Stovepipe boots

Gun belt worn loose not for a fast draw but for safety, to prevent buckle from digging into waist

1850s Texas saddle

Rowel spur

Texas cowboy of the late 1800s

Wooden stirrups are enclosed within the tapaderos

Brass spur, with buffalo head, Texas, 1914

Chap hook

Iron spur from South America, 1860s

Heel chain secures spur to boot

Steel trail spur from Texas, c. 1900

SPURRED ON!

Spurs were not intended to harm the horse, but to penetrate matted hair so the horse could feel the prod. A chap hook was an integral part of the metal shank to keep chaps or trousers from catching on the rowel.

Boots and spurs

COWBOYS TOOK CARE CHOOSING THEIR BOOTS – in the 1880s, custom-made boots cost $15, half a month's wages. The high, tapered heel ensured that the boot would not slip through the stirrup, and it could be dug into the ground when roping on foot (pp. 34–35). Western boots have remained popular, though their shape and style have changed a good deal. Today, many are not work boots, but fashion items. Because cowboys rarely groomed their horses, spurs were needed to penetrate the matted hair to prod the horse, though rowels were usually filed blunt.

Inlaid brand mark

Vamp (top of foot) made of shark skin

BIG EARS
The mule ears on these boots go from the top edge to overlap the heel.

Silver concha

BOOTS FOR BUCKAROOS
Tall so they can be worn with *armitas* (pp. 26–27), the boots have finger holes for pulling them on.

STOVEPIPE STYLE
Old-style "stovepipe" boots came up close to the knee to offer more protection. This pair dates from the 1880s or 1890s. The extreme underslung heel was just for fashion and must have made walking painful – as well as potentially dangerous!

Mexican inlaid silver spur

American, silver-plated, hand-forged spur

Plain nickel working spur

Neck of spur in form of female figure – in western spurs called a "gal-leg"

HISTORICAL SPURS
Spurs were brought to the Americas by Spanish settlers in the 1500s. Typically, they were large and heavy, traditionally made of silver mixed with iron, to create highly decorative spurs of great elegance. This Mexican style evolved in Texas and went north along the cattle trails to Kansas, Wyoming, and Montana (pp. 38–39).

SHORT AND SCALLOPED
The shorter boot with scalloped top is a modern style, probably deriving from the kind specially designed for early movie cowboys (pp. 60–61), like Tom Mix (1880–1940). These store-bought boots were made by Tony Lama of El Paso, Texas, in the 1970s. A former champion rodeo cowboy, Lama opened a boot factory on his retirement, and his products have become famous.

Diameter is 3.5 in (9 cm)

South American brass spur

Spanish American, hand-forged, bronze prick spur

Curved tip at end of 6.25-in (17-cm) long spur

Spanish American, hand-forged, engraved, iron prick spur

Tab sewn onto boot

V-shape gives extra space for tucking trousers into boots

Inlaid leather longhorn design, at both front and back

Large nickel rowel

Decorated leather spur strap

NO EXPENSE SPARED

The more lines of stitching on a boot, the more it costs. Stitching stiffens a boot and prevents it from wrinkling around the ankles. From the 1920s, colored leathers were added to provide decoration on boots, which made them even more expensive!

Mule ear

Stitching in blue, tan, yellow, and red

Calf made of soft latigo leather

IF THE BOOT FITS, WEAR IT
Custom-made boots fit superbly but are expensive, like this pair by Blucher, classic bootmakers in Oklahoma. However, cowboys used to soak new boots in water (while wearing them), and not take them off for days. The boots then took on the shape of the wearer's feet.

How to put on boots

Western boots obviously have neither laces nor buckles to fasten them. The only way they can grip the foot is to fit fairly tightly at the instep, while at the same time not being too slack at the heel. The best way to put on a boot is standing, stepping down into it, and hauling firmly on the pull-straps or mule-ears, while trying to avoid hopping about and cursing!

THESE BOOTS ARE MADE FOR RIDING
High, underslung heels made it difficult for cowboys to walk, but they were proud to show they had small feet. Pointed toes also made it easier to put feet into stirrups quickly.

Vamp made of tough bull hide

Traditional, California-style, silver spur with jinglebobs

Fancy silver concha

Buck-stitched spur strap

Ladies' western spur, c. 1900

Tiny rowel

Silver western spur, c. 1900

Brass rowel

Chap hook

Steel western spur, early 1900s

SPUR PARTS
A spur is made up of a heel band, a heel chain, a spur strap, and a spur button. A shank, which attaches the rowel to the heel band, can be straight, dropped, or raised (as worn by rodeo riders, pp. 62–63). However, California-style spurs show a great Mexican influence with solid buttons, drop shanks, an abundance of decorated silver, and jinglebobs.

MULE EARS
Mules were the frontier's beast of burden, famous for their stamina, stubbornness, and long ears. Because of their shape, the tabs for pulling on boots were promptly named "mule ears" by cowboys.

Chaps in "chaps"

RIDING HARD THROUGH THORNY BRUSH could rip a horseman's pants and legs! Mexican *vaqueros* (pp. 8–11) taught cowboys to protect themselves from the *chaparro prieto* (thornbrush) by wearing leather *chaparejos* (shortened to "chaps," pronounced "shaps"). Different styles emerged. Mexican *armitas* looked like a long, split apron, ending below the knee; "shotguns" and "batwings" were both ankle length and took their nicknames from their shapes. On northern ranges and on mountain slopes, chaps were usually made of Angora goat skin and were nicknamed "woolies." Chaps protected the rider from rain, cattle horns, horse bites, and chafed knees.

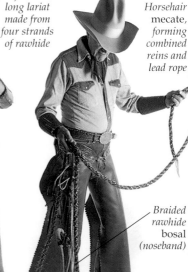

Back views of cowboys wearing *armitas* (left) and batwings (right)

Montana peak-style with distinctive dents

Fleece-lined waistcoat

Rawhide braiding on crown of Stetson

Denim bib-style shirt

Woolie chaps

American quarter used as concha

SHOTGUN-STYLE CHAPS
This modern 1980s cowboy is sporting shotgun chaps, that were made in California – the leather has been oiled to ensure that the chaps are waterproof. His "bib," or shield-fronted, shirt suggests he may be a fan of John Wayne, who wore them in many of his movies, although old-time cowboys would not have been likely to do so. This cowboy is enjoying his hobby of whittling a toy horse from a piece of wood.

Shotgun chaps with fringing down leg to keep the rain off

WINTER WOOLIES
This 1880s cowboy from Wyoming or Montana is dressed for the winter cold. His woolies are made of soft, curly, heavy buffalo hide and his expensive, linen bib shirt has been imported from the East. His Colt Lightning slide-action rifle can be fired very rapidly, but it needs constant cleaning and oiling, especially in winter, to prevent it from jamming.

ROMANTIC COWBOY
In this 1910 picture, a cowboy is wearing Angora goat chaps ("woolies"). By this date, the romantic image of the cowboy was hugely popular through the paintings of artists like Frederic Remington (1861–1909) and Charles Russell (1864–1926).

THREE KINDS OF CHAPS
These cowboys are wearing different kinds of chaps, which show how little the cowboys' clothing has changed since the 1860s. The cowboy on the left is wearing heavy leather chaps from Canada in the 1970s. His shirt is cotton, not wool, and he is wearing a "wild rag" (bandana). The center cowboy has on 1920s leather cuffs and *armitas* with a built-in waistband and open pockets on the thighs. He is holding a lariat (from the Spanish *la riata*). The cowboy on the right is wearing custom-made, batwing-style, heavy leather parade chaps, with scalloped edging. He is holding a hackamore (from the Spanish *jaquima*) headstall, or bridle, used for training horses up to five years old.

Buckle fastening on outside of leg

60-ft (18-m) long lariat made from four strands of rawhide

Horsehair mecate, forming combined reins and lead rope

Braided rawhide bosal (noseband)

Brand mark on chaps

Fringe on outside leg only

TWENTIETH-CENTURY COWBOY

This 1980s cowboy is wearing heavy leather, custom-made *armitas* (with a built-in waistband of the same material) over blue jeans. A long fringe, running around the bottom edge of the legs, is not just decoration, but is meant to drain away the rain.

High-crowned Stetson

Cotton shirt with popper buttons

Modern leather cuffs

Quirt made of braided strips of rawhide

1980s California cowboy

TEXAS COWBOY

These batwing chaps are worn by a Texas cowboy of the late 1800s. The silver conchas keep the ties from being pulled through the leather. No Stetson here, but an old-style, soft felt plainsman's hat. The stovepipe boots with underslung heel and rowel spurs are typical for a Texan. His revolver is an 1875 cartridge model, single-action .44 Remington, which some preferred to the less robust Colt .45 (pp. 46–47).

Hatband made of rope

Calfskin waistcoat

Rawhide quirt

Leather tie

Split-ear bridle

Bandanas were either spotted or print, as shown here

Striped cotton collarless shirt

Lariat made of braided latigo leather

Silver concha

Bottom hook traditionally left undone

Rowel spur

Underslung heel

1880s Texas cowboy

Life on a ranch

OUT ON THE GREAT GRASSLANDS, ranches had to be self-sufficient for long periods. In the late 1800s, American ranchers in the northern ranges might stock up on food and equipment for a year at a time. In Australia's outback (pp. 56–57), immense distances separated cattle stations and settlements, enforcing real isolation. Families were dependent on painfully slow camel and oxen trains for mail and supplies. The Flying Doctor service since 1928, School of the Air (learning by radio) since 1951, and modern roads have been important improvements in Australia. Ranches and cattle stations needed a water supply close by. Buildings, usually made of timber, were designed to adapt to changing needs and to meet the demands of the climate.

DON'T FENCE ME IN
Barbed wire, invented in 1874, was used by homesteaders in the U.S. to protect their crops, and by ranchers, too, particularly after 1885–1886, to fence off good pasture and water. Cowboys really hated the restrictions it brought and, even more, the new job of mending it.

WASTE NOT, WANT NOT
The horns and hide of cattle were made into a great variety of items – even household furniture, as shown by this chair from Kansas City.

Cowhide seat

Leg made from a longhorn's horn

HOME AND AWAY
When work with his livestock took a Camargue *gardian* far from his home (pp. 52–53), he would find shelter in a *cabane*, rather like an American cowboy's line camp (a small log cabin for overnight stays when away from ranch headquarters).

Cross to protect gardian in his home away from home

Brick chimney for stove used for both heating and cooking

Painted timber ranch house

Hitching rail for tying up horses

Bunkhouse made of logs

Shelf for holding a cowboy's shaving equipment

Chimney pipe to get rid of smoke from stove

"Dog trot"

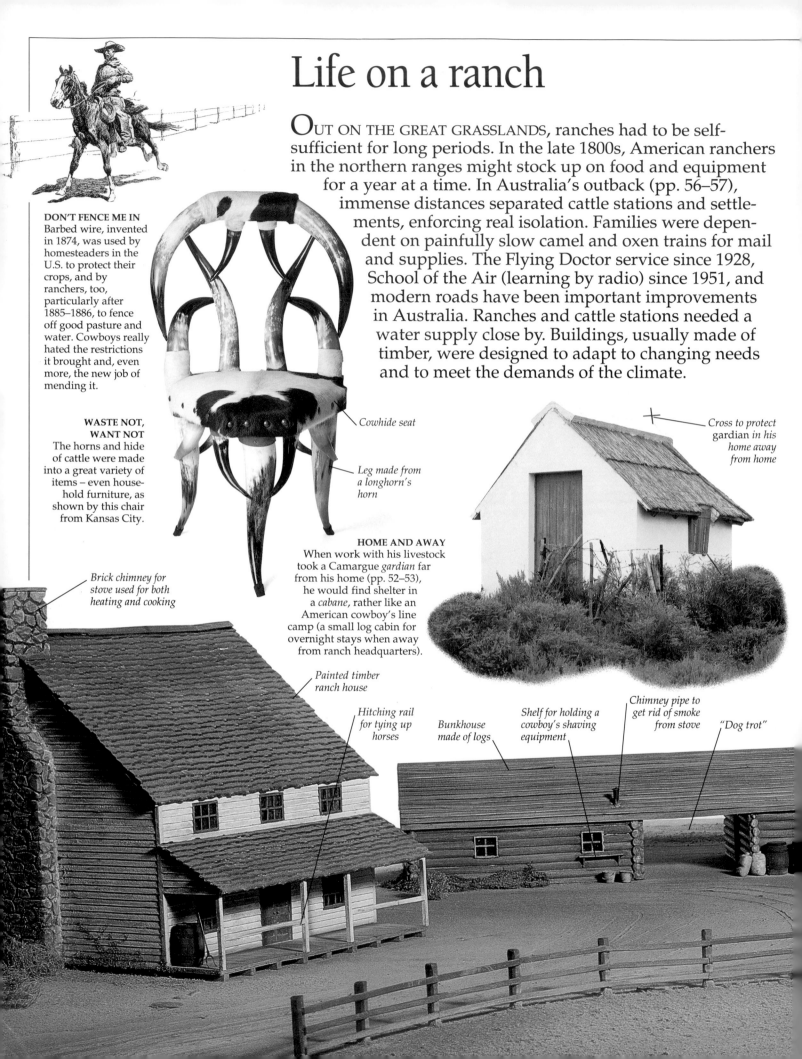

A MONGOLIAN PORTABLE CABIN
The herdsmen of the Mongolian steppes invented a dwelling that suited their seminomadic way of life. A *yurt* is a framework of poles, easily dismantled, covered with skins or woolen felt. The open fire vents its smoke through a central chimney.

A POOR *RANCHO*
Not all Argentine ranchers were rich *estancieros* (pp. 48–49). An English visitor in the 1890s, seeing their mud walls and roofs made of branches, mistook some *ranchos* for cattle shelters, but in fact they were dwellings for gauchos and their families.

IN THE OUTBACK
Like homesteads all over Australia, the buildings on a cattle station are low, rambling structures. They may have grown from a simple four-room, one-story house with an open-ended design. More bedrooms and living areas could be added as required.

Pages from mail-order catalogs were used to wallpaper the bunkhouses – the corset pages became a kind of pin-up calendar!

THE WISH BOOK
Mail order offered almost anything to people isolated on the range. Catalogs, like Bannerman's, were read eagerly, even by those who could not afford to buy.

DEEP IN THE HEART OF TEXAS
A Texas ranch house, copied all over the West, consisted of two log cabins connected by a "dog trot" (open hallway for cooling). This house became the cowboys' bunkhouse and cookhouse if the owner built a smarter, more expensive home. The timber-built barn stored horses' winter feed, and a windmill pumped water for people and animals alike.

Metal blade

Windmill draws water from artesian well (water found between two levels of hard rock under the earth's surface)

Pulley for lifting animal food to the upper floor of the barn

Snubbing post holds fast rope attached to horse being tamed in the corral

Ladder

Wooden fence keeps animals in the corral

Cookhouse with a timber roof

Tumble-weed

Water trough

Cattle and branding

PEOPLE HAVE REARED CATTLE for thousands of years, but it was the population explosion of the 19th century in Europe and America that turned cattle raising into an industry. Demand for meat encouraged ranching to spread across the world's great grasslands, so that it became an important enterprise in the U.S., Canada, Brazil, Argentina, and Australia. No cattle had existed in any of these countries before European settlers brought them. European cattle were originally hardy but lean. From the 1770s, however, a breeding revolution in Britain produced new, heavy beef strains like the Hereford, shorthorn, and Aberdeen angus. From the 1870s on, these were increasingly exported to replace or crossbreed with the old European longhorns in the New World. In Spain and in the Camargue in southern France, bulls are still bred solely for fighting.

WHERE THE BUFFALO ROAM
Up to the 1860s, millions of buffalo roamed the North American plains. In the mid-1870s they were ruthlessly slaughtered for their meat and skins by hunters. With cattle taking over their range, severe winters, and drought, buffalo nearly became extinct.

SUCCESS STORY
Herefords, with their distinctive red and white coloring, are considered to be the most successful of the beef breeds and are renowned for their hardiness, early maturity, and swift, efficient conversion of grass into meat. In the American West, they were imported from Britain into the northern ranges in the early 1880s and, crossbred with local cattle, they eventually replaced longhorns in Wyoming and Montana. With their ability to thrive anywhere, there are now more than five million pedigree Herefords in over 50 countries.

Typical white head of Hereford

TEXAS LONGHORNS
Descendants of Spanish cattle imported in the 1520s, longhorns spread from Mexico into the American West. Always half-wild, they were fierce and bad-tempered. Though poor quality beef – mostly muscle – they were very hardy and could survive on the sparse grass of the dry plains.

As well as its original brand, a calf had a road or trail brand added behind its left ear at the start of a cattle drive north from Texas.

Two branding irons from North America

MAKING A MARK
Branding was the easiest means for a rancher to identify the ownership of cattle roaming the open range. Marks, usually simple shapes or letters, or combinations such as Bar T (**– T**) or Circle B (**O B**), were burned through the hair into the surface of the animal's hide with red hot irons. Cowmen claimed this was relatively painless – cows probably thought otherwise!

This magnificent, 6-year-old prize-winning pedigree Hereford bull, named "Ironside," weighs 3,100 lb (1,400 kg) and stands 5 ft 6 in (1.7 m) at the flank.

DISPUTING A BRAND

Rustlers, or cattle thieves, tried various tricks to claim cattle. They branded over an existing mark or used a "running iron" (like a big iron poker) to change a brand. For example, Bar C would look like "–C" and could be changed easily to Lazy T Circle, " ⊢O" (where the "T" appears to be on its side). Originally, wandering "mavericks" (calves that had left their mothers) could be branded by whomever found them, but ranchers soon tried to stop this practice.

FRENCH MARKS

The fierce black bulls of the French Camargue are raised by local ranchers solely for the exciting and dangerous sport of the *course à la cocarde* (pp. 54–55). Each rancher separates the yearlings annually at the *ferrade*, or branding, and stamps them with their owner's mark – just as in the American West.

Branding irons from the French Camargue are used for both horses and bulls

BRITISH BLACK BULL

The Aberdeen angus was originally bred, as its name indicates, in Aberdeenshire in Scotland. This is a naturally hornless breed which matures quickly (so it is ready for market early). It yields a high proportion of high quality meat – some say it makes the best steaks. The breed was first introduced into the U.S. in 1873.

"Volvo," a 20-month-old, purebred Aberdeen angus bull by a Canadian sire

BY A SHORT HORN

Shorthorns, as shown in this 1890s engraving, were first bred in Durham county in England and became the most popular of the new breeds until they were replaced by the Hereford. They were exported to the U.S., Argentina, and Australia. In the U.S. the first shorthorn register was set up in 1846, and in Canada, in 1867. Shorthorns were brought to the northern ranges of the West during the 1870s.

Herefords usually have their horns removed (polling) when calves

"Emma" is a 6-month-old Hereford calf, sired by "Ironside"

CANNED MEAT

Most big American cities had meatpackers – firms preserving and packaging meat for transporting to market. Those buying western beef were centered in St. Louis, Kansas City, and above all Chicago. This New York company's absurd 1880s advertisement shows Mexican *vaqueros* on a New York dock.

31

Cutting cattle out of a herd

SEPARATING A SINGLE ANIMAL from a whole herd of uneasy cattle was a routine task at the roundup. Nevertheless, it took skill and a real partnership between horse and rider to deal with a dodging, panicky cow – the process was called "cutting out." It was necessary in order to remove strange cattle that had accidentally been gathered up, but mostly to brand yearlings and calves (pp. 30–31). Top-class cutting horses were much valued, and mustangs seemed to have instinctive "cow sense." With a little training, the most alert and intelligent horse could be pointed at the animal to be caught and would follow it through every twist and turn with hardly any use of the reins. One western story tells of a cutting horse that brought a jack-rabbit out of a herd!

FAST STOP
Stopping quickly from a gallop requires powerful braking! The "fast stop" is used both in cutting out and when roping (pp. 34–35). The horse brings the back legs forward, throws its weight back, braces its front legs, and skids to a stop. In reining pattern classes at western riding shows (above), the horse aims to complete a "sliding halt" within 25 to 30 ft (7.5–9 m).

1 SELECTING THE CALF
Horse and rider must begin cutting out quietly, so as not to alarm the herd, or indeed the animal selected, until as late as possible. The rider keeps a slack rein, and the horse has its eyes fixed on the target.

2 SEPARATING THE CALF
Once the target starts to run, a frantic dashing and dodging competition between horse and calf begins. The horse will try to keep itself between the calf and the herd to force the calf into the open and toward the branding fire.

Both rider and horse maintain eye contact with the calf during cutting

Quarter horse, "Dust My Tucker," is an excellent cutting horse – a 7-year-old female, 15.1 hands high (5 ft 1 in, 1.9 m)

Horse swings in one direction, but is poised to turn abruptly in the opposite direction if necessary

"CUTTIN' CRITTER"
Old-time cowboys did not seem to have given their horses much training, relying on those that showed natural intelligence and ability to learn cutting out by doing it. Today, horses can be trained by a "cutting critter" – a motorized plastic calf on rails that is moved quickly and changes direction abruptly.

MEXICAN-STYLE DRIVE
Some Spanish-American *vaqueros* (pp. 10–11) used brutal forms of training for their horses. To teach them obedience to the reins, horses would be blindfolded and run full tilt at a wall! These modern Mexican cowboys are chivying along some zebu cattle (pp. 50–51).

Horse assumes a threatening expression, with its ears laid back to intimidate the calf

GET OUT OF THAT
Western story magazines flourished after 1910, and their cover illustrations were often by well-known action artists. In search of excitement, this artist has his cowboy in serious difficulties. Hopefully, his horse will know what to do – because the rider obviously does not!

Loose reins allow horse to follow its instinct with no instruction from the rider

Rider's feet, as well as legs and body, give clear signals to horse when it is working

Calf is mix of Hereford and Aberdeen angus breeds

3 TURNING THE CALF
Once in the open, the target animal will make desperate attempts to get back to the herd – wheeling, balking, and ducking behind the horse. The best cutting horses can stop short from a gallop and immediately sprint off in a new direction. Riders must stay in balance with their horses, or they will be thrown.

WHICH WAY NEXT?
This is how the target appears to the cutting horse – small, stubborn, and agile. This calf is a Hereford–Aberdeen angus cross, but no less trouble for it.

33

Continued on next page

THE FINE ART OF ROPING
Roping was a skill so impressive that it became entertainment. Cowboys in Buffalo Bill's Wild West show (pp. 60–61) demonstrated roping tricks, and after 1900, roping acts in vaudeville (theatrical) shows became popular. For many years, the much-loved entertainer Will Rogers (1870–1935) combined trick roping with comedy in his stage act.

South American lariat made of rawhide

Early sisal rope made of braided hemp (c. 1890s)

Modern western rope made of hemp

EITHER HIDE OR HAIR – OR GRASS
Originally, cowboys copied Mexican *vaqueros'* braided rawhide lariats, widely used throughout Spanish America. Then they adopted the braided, grass rope, or one made from sisal (the stiff fibers of the Mexican agave plant). Modern ropes are made from nylon, or a mixture of man-made fibers and grass.

The cowboy holds the "piggin' string" between his teeth in a rodeo event

Hondo, or eyelet

Catch rope is thrown around calf's head in a rodeo event

TAKING AIM
For a small calf, a working cowboy would use a heel catch, casting sideways to slip the rope under the animal's hind legs. It could then be dragged conveniently to the branding fire.

CAUGHT SHORT
Mexican *vaqueros* taught American cowboys their trade (pp. 10–11). It was they who first perfected skills with the lariat (*la reata*) and developed roping techniques for dealing with range cattle and horses.

In a rodeo event, calf is roped around its head – its feet are tied with a "piggin' string" (made from fine rope)

Horse wears protective boots on its legs during a rodeo event

LOOP THE LOOP
Old-time Mongolian herdsmen did not develop a rope for capturing wild horses. Instead they invented an ingenious long pole with a noose at the end to slip over the horse's head. Manipulating pole and noose must have required as much skill as using a lariat.

IT TAKES TWO
For roping cattle, a cowboy needs only two basic throws. A "head" catch is thrown around the horns (around the neck might strangle the beast), while a "heel" catch is aimed at the back legs to trip it.

Using a lariat

One end of the 40-ft (12-m) long lariat, or rope, is slipped through the honda, or eyelet, to make a large loop. A right-handed cowboy holds the loop (with the honda partway down) and part of the rope in his right hand, while the rest of the rope is coiled in his left hand. Whirling it only a couple of times to gain momentum, the cowboy flings the loop at the target. The stiff rope fiber keeps the loop flat and open until jerked tight.

EL RODEO STAR
Roping became one of the basic events in rodeo riding – as shown in this 1924 sketch by artist Charles Simpson.

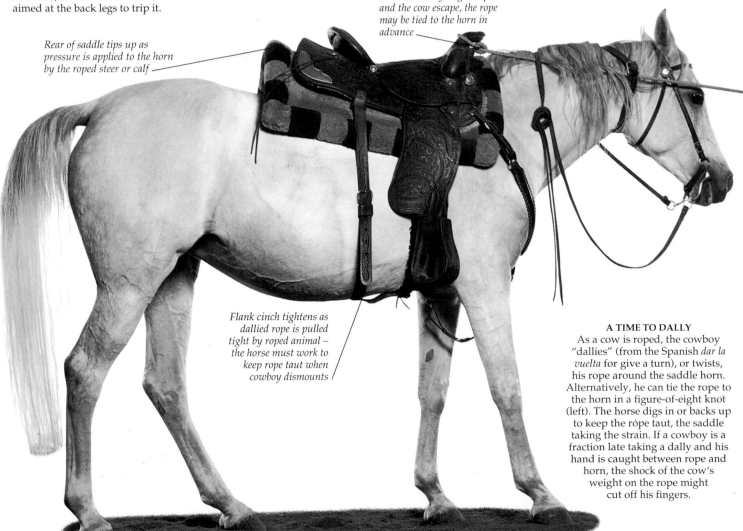

Because a dally might slip and the cow escape, the rope may be tied to the horn in advance

Rear of saddle tips up as pressure is applied to the horn by the roped steer or calf

Flank cinch tightens as dallied rope is pulled tight by roped animal – the horse must work to keep rope taut when cowboy dismounts

A TIME TO DALLY
As a cow is roped, the cowboy "dallies" (from the Spanish *dar la vuelta* for give a turn), or twists, his rope around the saddle horn. Alternatively, he can tie the rope to the horn in a figure-of-eight knot (left). The horse digs in or backs up to keep the rope taut, the saddle taking the strain. If a cowboy is a fraction late taking a dally and his hand is caught between rope and horn, the shock of the cow's weight on the rope might cut off his fingers.

Home on the range

ON THE TRAIL OR AT ROUNDUP, the camp cook was king. Hungry cowboys ached for hot food and no one dared criticize the man who prepared it. His chuck wagon was a self-contained larder and kitchen. A set of drawers held basics like flour, lard, and coffee, and luxuries like dried apples and raisins. The body of the wagon carried bedrolls and spare equipment. Food was prepared on a fold-down shelf at the rear. It was usually "sowbelly" (bacon), beans, and bread (made up as a batter and fried). Meat spoiled quickly, despite the tons of beef on hand. Jackrabbits, "prairie chickens" (a kind of grouse), and, in Wyoming, antelope were shot for the pot.

Large, metal hoop could be covered with canvas if weather became hot or rainy

Driver's seat

Hand brake

Lesser prairie chicken lived in semidesert terrain

Wagon bed for bulk storage

FOOD ON THE RUN
Cooks who took pride in their work were always looking for extra meat to relieve the monotony of bacon. The trouble was, edible wildlife on the trail (pp. 38–39) moved fast! Prairie chickens and jackrabbits (killed with a shotgun) and antelope (a long-range rifle shot) made a fine stew.

Jackrabbits were found east of California across the prairies

Antelope were really small pronghorned deer

Front wheel smaller than back wheel makes turning easier

Spare rope

Water barrel

Desperate Dan – a famous cartoon cowboy character

Cow pie

Metal tag also with bull logo

Famous label with a bull on every pack

DESPERATE DAN
Created by cartoonist Dudley D. Watkins in 1937, Desperate Dan of Cactusville demolished entire saloons and then would tuck into a cow pie!

SETTING THE WEST ON FIRE
Some cowboys chewed tobacco, but those who smoked despised "tailor mades" and rolled their own. Bull Durham tobacco came in 5-cent muslin sacks – and the papers were free!

Bull Durham tobacco

CHUCK WAGON SPECIAL
The first design for a chuck wagon was made by cattleman Charles Goodnight in 1866, when he adapted an old army wagon. He added four pieces of equipment – a barrel to hold two days' supply of water, a heavy tool box, hoops for a protective canvas, and, most important of all, a chuck box.

Chuck box (set of drawers) containing cook's basic necessities – flour, coffee, beans, sugar, and even grain for the wagon team

Metal lantern, with handle

Skillet

Coffee cup

Bedroll

CHOW'S UP!
Cowboy meals were no picnic! The food was boring and unhealthy, and cooks were often "stove-up" (injured) former cowboys with no skills. Hygiene was non existent – cups and plates were thrown into the "wreck pan" and just scoured with sand if water was not plentiful. It is hardly surprising that cowboys, when they got to town (pp. 42–43), spent their money on eggs and steaks, as well as liquor.

Tools, such as a shovel, ax, branding irons, and horseshoe equipment, were stored in a tool box (under chuck box)

Dried fruit

Useful extra hook

Metal plate

Brake for rear wheel

"Wreck pan"

Large cooking pot for cooking stews over an open campfire

Support for hinged lid of chuck box swings down to form work table for the cook

Apron made from old canvas bag

A LONG AND WINDING TRAIL
A herd of 2,500 cattle might stretch a mile along the trail, tended by 15 cowboys choking on the dust, as shown in this 1870s engraving of a cattle drive from Texas to Abilene.

On the trail drive

Driving cattle a thousand miles across dangerous country made a business venture into an epic. In the U.S., eastern cities were hungry for beef, five million Texas cattle roamed wild, and the railroads linked the West with Chicago meat packers – all this created the first trail drives. As the "beef bonanza" spread ranching north in 1880–1881, cattle were driven all the way to Wyoming, Montana, and the Dakotas. The advance of railroads into south Texas and overstocking in the northwest ended the drives in the early 1880s. In Australia, overlanders seeking new pastures pioneered stock routes (trails) through uncharted country sometimes defended by hostile Aborigines. In 1883, 8,000 cattle were driven a record 2,500 miles (4,000 km)!

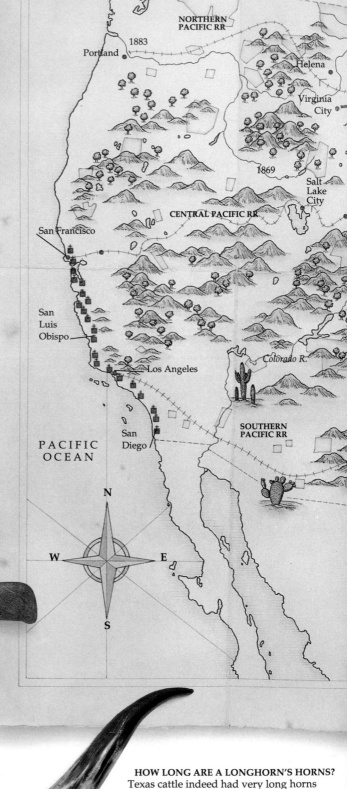

Two bowie-style knives, c. 1900

Bone handle

Blood groove in steel blade

Wooden handle

DANGEROUS KNIVES
Made popular by the Texas adventurer Colonel James Bowie (1799–1836), the bowie (pronounced *boowie*) knife was a formidable weapon. Most cowboys carried an all-purpose knife; although the bowie knife was intended for fighting, it was also used by hunters.

Set of longhorn's horns measuring 5 ft (1.5 m) from tip to tip

HOW LONG ARE A LONGHORN'S HORNS?
Texas cattle indeed had very long horns – a spread of 5 ft (1.5 m) was common! Descendants of Iberian cattle brought by the Spaniards (pp. 30–31), longhorns had been left to breed untended during the Civil War (1861–1865). Cowboys knew that longhorns were truly wild beasts – fierce, mean-tempered, and dangerous – and that a herd was trouble waiting to happen (pp. 40–41).

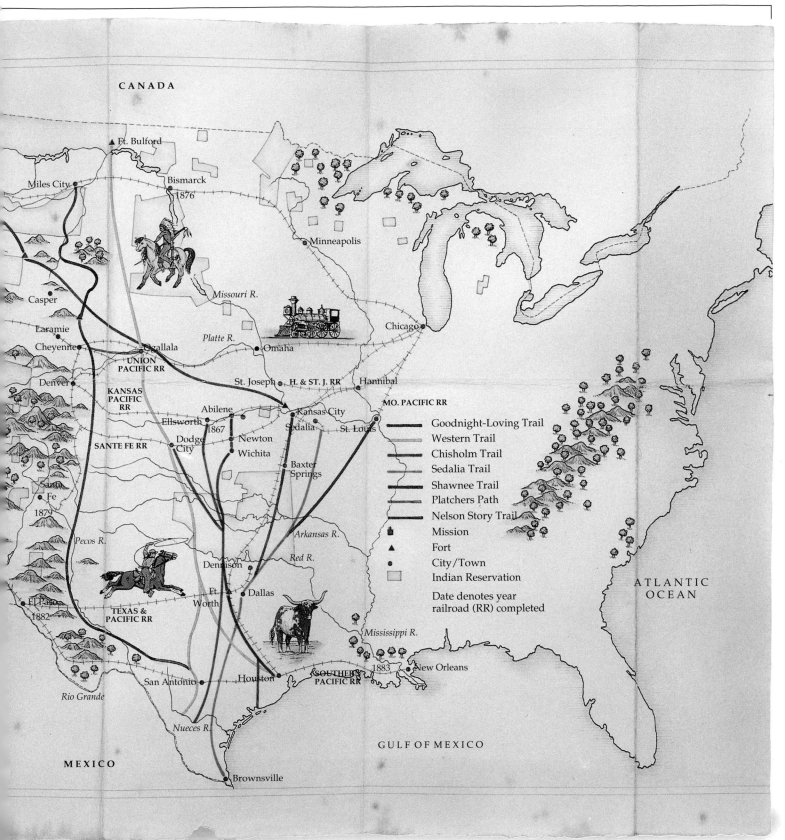

CANADA

▲ Ft. Bulford

Miles City •

Bismarck
1876

Minneapolis •

Missouri R.

Casper •

Laramie •
Cheyenne •
Ogallala •

Platte R.

Omaha •

Chicago •

UNION
PACIFIC RR

St. Joseph •   H. & ST. J. RR   Hannibal •

Denver •

KANSAS
PACIFIC
RR

MO. PACIFIC RR

Abilene •
Ellsworth •   Kansas City ▲
1867   Sedalia •   St. Louis •
Dodge
City •   Newton •
Wichita •

SANTE FE RR

Baxter
Springs •

Santa
Fe •

Arkansas R.

1879

Pecos R.   *Red R.*

Dennison •

Ft. ▲   Dallas •
Worth

El Paso •

1882

TEXAS &
PACIFIC RR

San Antonio •   Houston •

1883   New Orleans •

Rio Grande

SOUTHERN
PACIFIC RR

Nueces R.

ATLANTIC
OCEAN

Brownsville •

MEXICO

GULF OF MEXICO

Legend

━━━ Goodnight-Loving Trail
━━━ Western Trail
━━━ Chisholm Trail
━━━ Sedalia Trail
━━━ Shawnee Trail
━━━ Platchers Path
━━━ Nelson Story Trail
▮ Mission
▲ Fort
• City/Town
▢ Indian Reservation

Date denotes year
railroad (RR) completed

WET WEATHER
Trailing a herd in
a northwest
winter was
miserable
work! Oilskin
slickers were
the only protection
against rain and snow.

NORTHWARD HO!
Jesse Chisholm
(1806–1868) laid out
a supply route from
Texas to Kansas
during the
Civil War – it
later became a
trail for herds
heading to
Abilene.

EPIC JOURNEYS
Cattle trails linked ranges with railroads. In 1866
fear of Texas fever infecting local cattle closed the
Missouri border and the trails that led there. The
alternative Chisholm Trail carried two million
cattle up to the Kansas railheads between 1867 and
1871. In the 1870s, the Western Trail ran directly to
Dodge City. Named after two ranchers, the
Goodnight-Loving Trail was laid out in 1866 to
supply Colorado mining camps, but was soon used
to stock the ranges of Wyoming and Montana.

Continued on next page

Continued from previous page

Dangers on the trail

A trail drive was not fun – it was hours of stupefying boredom interspersed with moments of acute danger. Cowboys rarely saw hostile Indians. Mostly they rode the flanks of a herd to keep cows from wandering off, while the "drag rider" at the rear, choking on dust, chivied stragglers. The main worry was finding water at the end of the day. But range cattle were easily alarmed, "ornery" (mean-tempered), and not very smart. At a river crossing they might not only drown themselves but, in panic, a cowboy too. The biggest threat was a stampede, where a second's mistake in a sea of tossing horns and pounding hooves was a death sentence.

STAMPEDE!
Cattle were mindlessly nervous. A herd might be spooked by any unexpected sight, a sudden noise, or unusual scent – certainly lightning would terrorize them! The animals would then, without warning, burst into a stampede, running for miles. The cowboys' only hope was to race to the head of the herd and, by firing pistols, waving hats, and yelling, frighten the leaders into turning until the whole herd began to "mill," or circle, aimlessly.

Starr .44 revolver (1858) was one of the first double-action, or self-cocking, models

Nipple

Soft cap

Walnut grip

Colt model 1851 Navy .36 revolver

Tin holding percussion caps

Flask containing gunpowder

PACKING A PISTOL
Cowboys used their revolvers mostly to deal with the dangers on the trail. They might need to shoot a fatally injured horse, a maddened steer, or a rattlesnake. Pistols were fired in the air to turn a stampeding herd or give the traditional distress signal (three shots).

FOOD ON THE HOOF
Grizzly bears saw horses and cattle as food. Ferocious, 8 ft (2.4 m) in height, and weighing up to 800 lb (365 kg), grizzlies were an infrequent but serious hazard. These teeth belonged to a grizzly shot in British Columbia, Canada, after killing livestock. The rifle cartridge shows how big the teeth were.

CRY WOLF
The American timber wolf was a serious problem to ranchers. Wolves were not a threat to people, but after the buffalo had been wiped out, they preyed on calves and colts. They were killed by traps or poisoned with bait laced with strychnine.

NOT A CUDDLY TOY!
Brown bears ranged across America wherever the country was wild, mountainous, or forested. They were omnivores (eating animals and plants) and learned to add calves to their diet. Up to 6 ft (1.8 m) long and weighing 200 to 500 lb (90–250 kg), they were dangerous if alarmed.

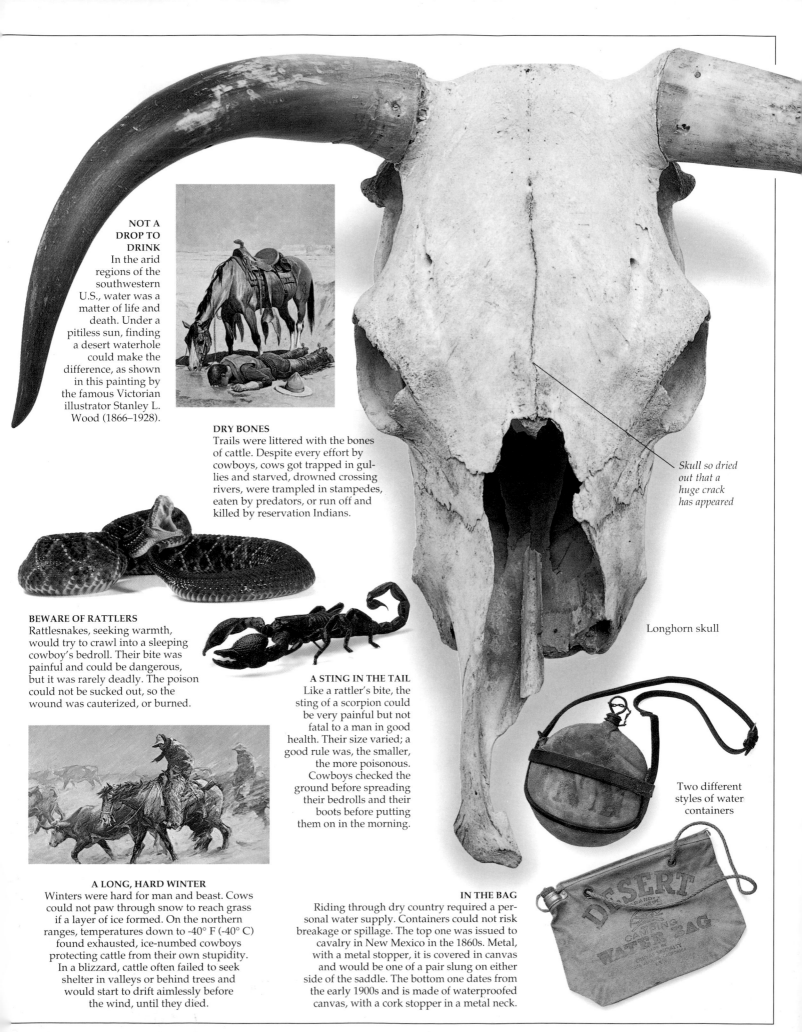

NOT A DROP TO DRINK
In the arid regions of the southwestern U.S., water was a matter of life and death. Under a pitiless sun, finding a desert waterhole could make the difference, as shown in this painting by the famous Victorian illustrator Stanley L. Wood (1866–1928).

DRY BONES
Trails were littered with the bones of cattle. Despite every effort by cowboys, cows got trapped in gullies and starved, drowned crossing rivers, were trampled in stampedes, eaten by predators, or run off and killed by reservation Indians.

Skull so dried out that a huge crack has appeared

BEWARE OF RATTLERS
Rattlesnakes, seeking warmth, would try to crawl into a sleeping cowboy's bedroll. Their bite was painful and could be dangerous, but it was rarely deadly. The poison could not be sucked out, so the wound was cauterized, or burned.

A STING IN THE TAIL
Like a rattler's bite, the sting of a scorpion could be very painful but not fatal to a man in good health. Their size varied; a good rule was, the smaller, the more poisonous. Cowboys checked the ground before spreading their bedrolls and their boots before putting them on in the morning.

Longhorn skull

Two different styles of water containers

A LONG, HARD WINTER
Winters were hard for man and beast. Cows could not paw through snow to reach grass if a layer of ice formed. On the northern ranges, temperatures down to -40° F (-40° C) found exhausted, ice-numbed cowboys protecting cattle from their own stupidity. In a blizzard, cattle often failed to seek shelter in valleys or behind trees and would start to drift aimlessly before the wind, until they died.

IN THE BAG
Riding through dry country required a personal water supply. Containers could not risk breakage or spillage. The top one was issued to cavalry in New Mexico in the 1860s. Metal, with a metal stopper, it is covered in canvas and would be one of a pair slung on either side of the saddle. The bottom one dates from the early 1900s and is made of waterproofed canvas, with a cork stopper in a metal neck.

Law and order

STEELY-EYED LAWMEN, fast on the draw, kept the peace on Hollywood's frontier. In the real West things were usually less exciting. Sometimes, in addition to law enforcement, an elected county sheriff collected local taxes. Town marshals, usually appointed by the city council, were expected to enforce health and safety regulations, collect license fees, and serve warrants. In some towns these jobs offered power and opportunity to make money. Only in cow towns and mining communities, and only while conditions required it, were law officers gunmen.

SHOOT-OUT
Street gunfights were not as common as westerns suggest. Remington's drawing may be based on the shoot-out between Luke Short and Jim Courtright at Fort Worth, Texas, in 1887.

Sheriff's jail keys

Marshal's badge made of silver (c. 1870)

Deputy's badge made of silver (1897)

DEPUTY LAWMAN
Shady characters as well as honest lawmen could become deputy marshals – Virgil Earp (1843–1906) held this post in Arizona in 1879.

MARSHAL OF DEADWOOD
The marshal of Deadwood, a mining town in Dakota Territory, had to deal with frequent stage robberies and the murder of Wild Bill Hickok (1837–1876).

"JAILBIRD"
The death penalty was unusual in the West. Prison, like the Yuma penitentiary in Arizona Territory, was the fate of many badmen. Here is an example of a 1900s prison guard's brass badge.

Special agent's badge, made of nickel

PAINTING THE TOWN RED
After three months or more on the trail (pp. 38–39), Texas cowboys quickly spent their hard-earned money in the cow towns of Kansas on liquor, gambling, and women. Even in good humor they might shoot up the town and, if unchecked, they readily turned to serious violence. Strong law enforcement was demanded by respectable citizens. Wichita (above) had seven marshals from 1868 to 1871 – all ineffective until the firm rule of Michael Meager (1871–1874) brought order.

  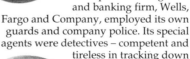

Bank guard's badge, made of nickel

Railroad police badge, made of nickel

SPECIAL AGENTS
The powerful stage line and banking firm, Wells, Fargo and Company, employed its own guards and company police. Its special agents were detectives – competent and tireless in tracking down those who preyed on it.

  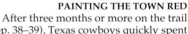

Pinkerton badge (1860)

TEXAS RANGERS FOREVER
First formed in 1835, the Texas Rangers were reformed in 1873 into a frontier battalion to deal with Indians, bandits, and rustlers. Since 1935, the Rangers have been part of the Texas Department of Public Safety.

THE PINKERTON AGENT
The Pinkerton Detective Agency was a formidable private organization. It was detested in the West for bombing the James family (pp. 44–45) home in 1875 and for breaking miners' strikes in the 1880s.

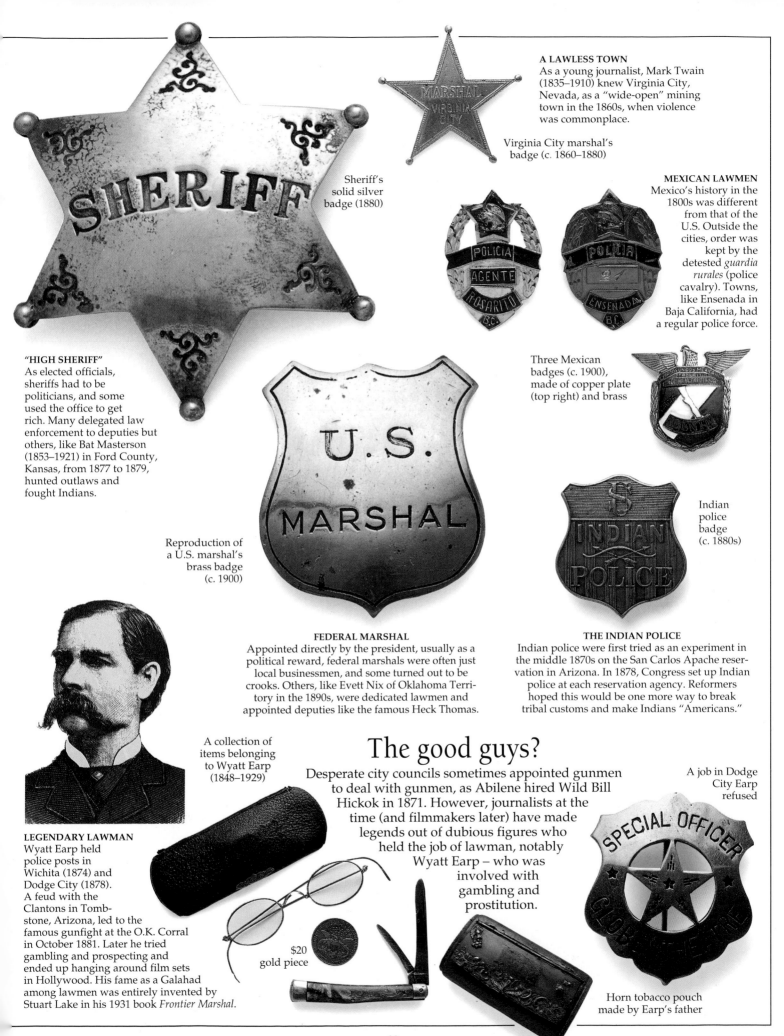

Sheriff's solid silver badge (1880)

As a young journalist, Mark Twain (1835–1910) knew Virginia City, Nevada, as a "wide-open" mining town in the 1860s, when violence was commonplace.

Virginia City marshal's badge (c. 1860–1880)

MEXICAN LAWMEN
Mexico's history in the 1800s was different from that of the U.S. Outside the cities, order was kept by the detested *guardia rurales* (police cavalry). Towns, like Ensenada in Baja California, had a regular police force.

"HIGH SHERIFF"
As elected officials, sheriffs had to be politicians, and some used the office to get rich. Many delegated law enforcement to deputies but others, like Bat Masterson (1853–1921) in Ford County, Kansas, from 1877 to 1879, hunted outlaws and fought Indians.

Three Mexican badges (c. 1900), made of copper plate (top right) and brass

Reproduction of a U.S. marshal's brass badge (c. 1900)

Indian police badge (c. 1880s)

FEDERAL MARSHAL
Appointed directly by the president, usually as a political reward, federal marshals were often just local businessmen, and some turned out to be crooks. Others, like Evett Nix of Oklahoma Territory in the 1890s, were dedicated lawmen and appointed deputies like the famous Heck Thomas.

THE INDIAN POLICE
Indian police were first tried as an experiment in the middle 1870s on the San Carlos Apache reservation in Arizona. In 1878, Congress set up Indian police at each reservation agency. Reformers hoped this would be one more way to break tribal customs and make Indians "Americans."

A collection of items belonging to Wyatt Earp (1848–1929)

The good guys?

Desperate city councils sometimes appointed gunmen to deal with gunmen, as Abilene hired Wild Bill Hickok in 1871. However, journalists at the time (and filmmakers later) have made legends out of dubious figures who held the job of lawman, notably Wyatt Earp – who was involved with gambling and prostitution.

A job in Dodge City Earp refused

LEGENDARY LAWMAN
Wyatt Earp held police posts in Wichita (1874) and Dodge City (1878). A feud with the Clantons in Tombstone, Arizona, led to the famous gunfight at the O.K. Corral in October 1881. Later he tried gambling and prospecting and ended up hanging around film sets in Hollywood. His fame as a Galahad among lawmen was entirely invented by Stuart Lake in his 1931 book *Frontier Marshal*.

$20 gold piece

Horn tobacco pouch made by Earp's father

Guns and gunslingers

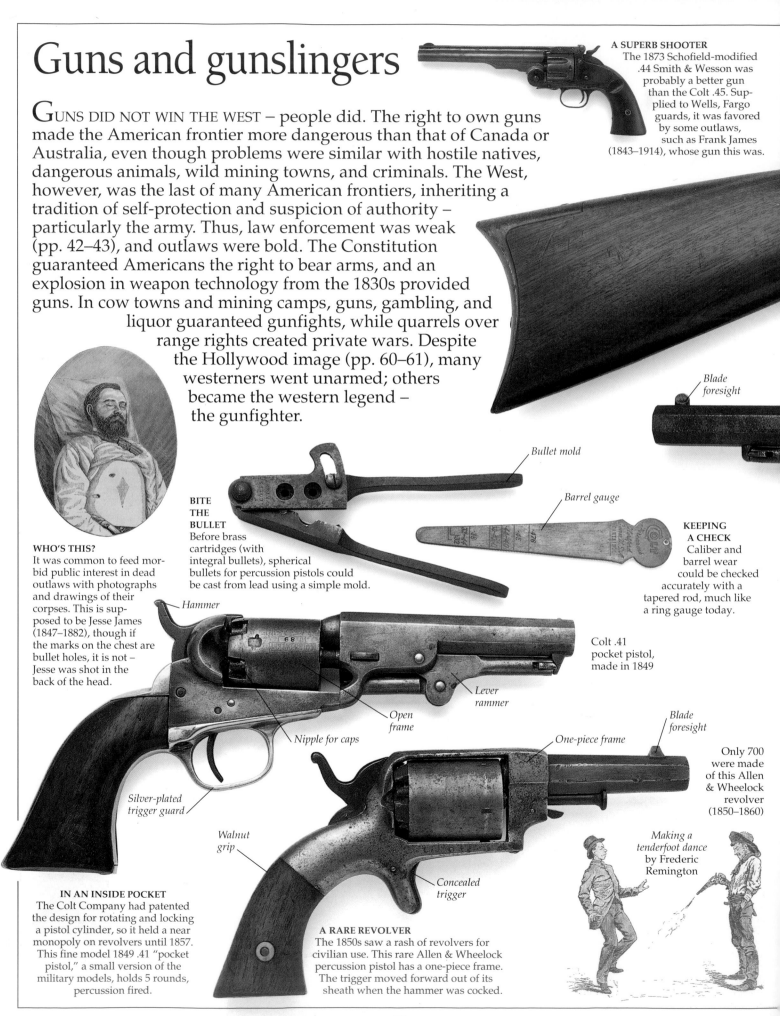

GUNS DID NOT WIN THE WEST – people did. The right to own guns made the American frontier more dangerous than that of Canada or Australia, even though problems were similar with hostile natives, dangerous animals, wild mining towns, and criminals. The West, however, was the last of many American frontiers, inheriting a tradition of self-protection and suspicion of authority – particularly the army. Thus, law enforcement was weak (pp. 42–43), and outlaws were bold. The Constitution guaranteed Americans the right to bear arms, and an explosion in weapon technology from the 1830s provided guns. In cow towns and mining camps, guns, gambling, and liquor guaranteed gunfights, while quarrels over range rights created private wars. Despite the Hollywood image (pp. 60–61), many westerners went unarmed; others became the western legend – the gunfighter.

A SUPERB SHOOTER
The 1873 Schofield-modified .44 Smith & Wesson was probably a better gun than the Colt .45. Supplied to Wells, Fargo guards, it was favored by some outlaws, such as Frank James (1843–1914), whose gun this was.

Blade foresight

Bullet mold

Barrel gauge

BITE THE BULLET
Before brass cartridges (with integral bullets), spherical bullets for percussion pistols could be cast from lead using a simple mold.

KEEPING A CHECK
Caliber and barrel wear could be checked accurately with a tapered rod, much like a ring gauge today.

WHO'S THIS?
It was common to feed morbid public interest in dead outlaws with photographs and drawings of their corpses. This is supposed to be Jesse James (1847–1882), though if the marks on the chest are bullet holes, it is not – Jesse was shot in the back of the head.

Hammer

Colt .41 pocket pistol, made in 1849

Lever rammer

Open frame

Nipple for caps

Silver-plated trigger guard

Blade foresight

One-piece frame

Only 700 were made of this Allen & Wheelock revolver (1850–1860)

Walnut grip

Concealed trigger

IN AN INSIDE POCKET
The Colt Company had patented the design for rotating and locking a pistol cylinder, so it held a near monopoly on revolvers until 1857. This fine model 1849 .41 "pocket pistol," a small version of the military models, holds 5 rounds, percussion fired.

A RARE REVOLVER
The 1850s saw a rash of revolvers for civilian use. This rare Allen & Wheelock percussion pistol has a one-piece frame. The trigger moved forward out of its sheath when the hammer was cocked.

Making a tenderfoot dance by Frederic Remington

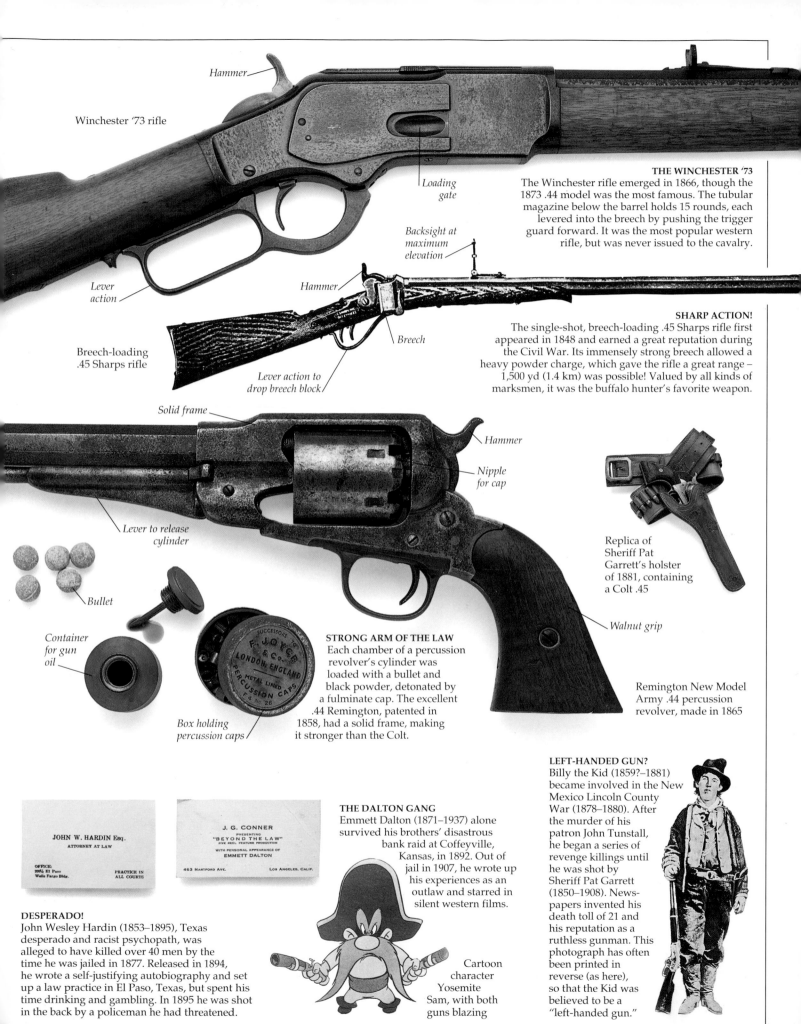

Hammer

Winchester '73 rifle

Loading gate

THE WINCHESTER '73
The Winchester rifle emerged in 1866, though the 1873 .44 model was the most famous. The tubular magazine below the barrel holds 15 rounds, each levered into the breech by pushing the trigger guard forward. It was the most popular western rifle, but was never issued to the cavalry.

Lever action

Backsight at maximum elevation

Hammer

Breech-loading .45 Sharps rifle

Breech

Lever action to drop breech block

SHARP ACTION!
The single-shot, breech-loading .45 Sharps rifle first appeared in 1848 and earned a great reputation during the Civil War. Its immensely strong breech allowed a heavy powder charge, which gave the rifle a great range – 1,500 yd (1.4 km) was possible! Valued by all kinds of marksmen, it was the buffalo hunter's favorite weapon.

Solid frame

Hammer

Nipple for cap

Lever to release cylinder

Bullet

Container for gun oil

F. JOYCE & Co. LONDON, ENGLAND METAL LINED PERCUSSION CAPS

Box holding percussion caps

Replica of Sheriff Pat Garrett's holster of 1881, containing a Colt .45

Walnut grip

STRONG ARM OF THE LAW
Each chamber of a percussion revolver's cylinder was loaded with a bullet and black powder, detonated by a fulminate cap. The excellent .44 Remington, patented in 1858, had a solid frame, making it stronger than the Colt.

Remington New Model Army .44 percussion revolver, made in 1865

JOHN W. HARDIN Esq.
ATTORNEY AT LAW

OFFICE:
200½ El Paso
Wells Fargo Bldg.

PRACTICE IN
ALL COURTS

J. G. CONNER
PRESENTING
"BEYOND THE LAW"
FIVE REEL FEATURE PRODUCTION
WITH PERSONAL APPEARANCE OF
EMMETT DALTON

463 HARTFORD AVE.   Los Angeles, Calif.

THE DALTON GANG
Emmett Dalton (1871–1937) alone survived his brothers' disastrous bank raid at Coffeyville, Kansas, in 1892. Out of jail in 1907, he wrote up his experiences as an outlaw and starred in silent western films.

LEFT-HANDED GUN?
Billy the Kid (1859?–1881) became involved in the New Mexico Lincoln County War (1878–1880). After the murder of his patron John Tunstall, he began a series of revenge killings until he was shot by Sheriff Pat Garrett (1850–1908). Newspapers invented his death toll of 21 and his reputation as a ruthless gunman. This photograph has often been printed in reverse (as here), so that the Kid was believed to be a "left-handed gun."

DESPERADO!
John Wesley Hardin (1853–1895), Texas desperado and racist psychopath, was alleged to have killed over 40 men by the time he was jailed in 1877. Released in 1894, he wrote a self-justifying autobiography and set up a law practice in El Paso, Texas, but spent his time drinking and gambling. In 1895 he was shot in the back by a policeman he had threatened.

Cartoon character Yosemite Sam, with both guns blazing

Six gun

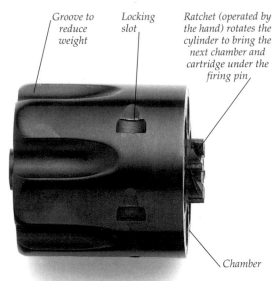

THE 1873 COLT single-action Army revolver has one real claim to fame – in the West it probably killed more people than any other. When production was suspended in 1941, 357,859 had been sold. In 1878, the .45 Peacemaker model was supplemented by the Frontier – its .44 caliber cartridge also fitted the Winchester rifle (pp. 44–45). Such large caliber pistols – heavy (2 lb 4oz, or 1 kg) to absorb the recoil – had guaranteed stopping power. The Colt was accurate, well balanced, and could be fired even if parts of the mechanism broke, which happened often.

Groove to reduce weight

Locking slot

Ratchet (operated by the hand) rotates the cylinder to bring the next chamber and cartridge under the firing pin

Chamber

Cylinder

Shield deflects gas that escapes when gun is fired

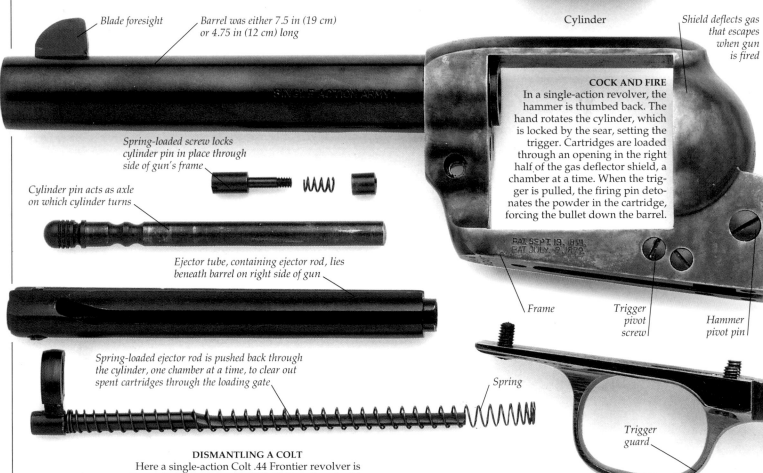

Blade foresight

Barrel was either 7.5 in (19 cm) or 4.75 in (12 cm) long

COCK AND FIRE
In a single-action revolver, the hammer is thumbed back. The hand rotates the cylinder, which is locked by the sear, setting the trigger. Cartridges are loaded through an opening in the right half of the gas deflector shield, a chamber at a time. When the trigger is pulled, the firing pin detonates the powder in the cartridge, forcing the bullet down the barrel.

Spring-loaded screw locks cylinder pin in place through side of gun's frame

Cylinder pin acts as axle on which cylinder turns

Ejector tube, containing ejector rod, lies beneath barrel on right side of gun

Frame

Trigger pivot screw

Hammer pivot pin

Spring-loaded ejector rod is pushed back through the cylinder, one chamber at a time, to clear out spent cartridges through the loading gate

Spring

Trigger guard

DISMANTLING A COLT
Here a single-action Colt .44 Frontier revolver is dismantled. However, in 1878, Colt made a double-action revolver – the Lightning, in .38 or .44 caliber. In this type of self-cocking weapon, a firm pull on the trigger alone lifted the hammer (and rotated the cylinder and locked it) and let it fall.

TRIGGER ACTION
When the hammer is cocked, the sear sets the trigger on its spring to trip the hammer. It also locks the cylinder, so that the next cartridge is in line with the barrel and under the firing pin. Although the lock mechanism was an original Colt patent, it was notorious for breaking, especially the trigger spring.

Trigger sear and cylinder stop

Trigger spring

Trigger connected to hammer by trigger spring and sear

THE WALKER COLT
In 1847, the U.S. Army sent Captain Samuel Walker to buy Colt revolvers. Walker suggested several improvements and the new gun became known as the "Walker Colt." Though huge – 15.5 in (39 cm) long and weighing 4.5 lb (2 kg) – it was the basis for all future Colt designs until 1873.

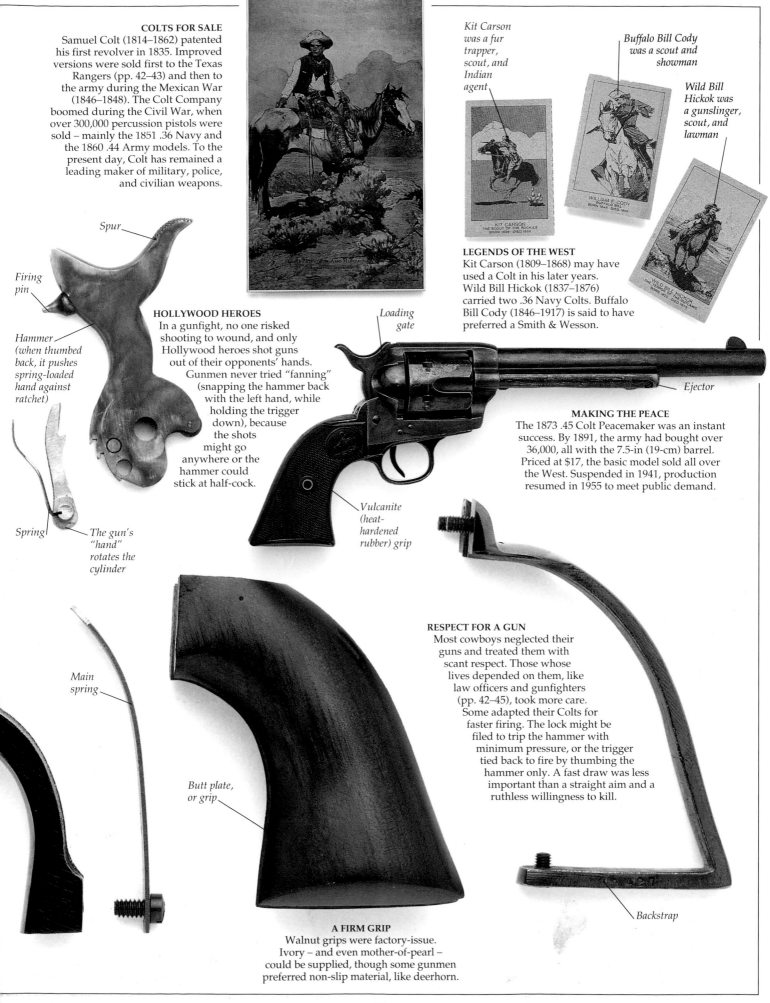

COLTS FOR SALE
Samuel Colt (1814–1862) patented his first revolver in 1835. Improved versions were sold first to the Texas Rangers (pp. 42–43) and then to the army during the Mexican War (1846–1848). The Colt Company boomed during the Civil War, when over 300,000 percussion pistols were sold – mainly the 1851 .36 Navy and the 1860 .44 Army models. To the present day, Colt has remained a leading maker of military, police, and civilian weapons.

Kit Carson was a fur trapper, scout, and Indian agent

Buffalo Bill Cody was a scout and showman

Wild Bill Hickok was a gunslinger, scout, and lawman

LEGENDS OF THE WEST
Kit Carson (1809–1868) may have used a Colt in his later years. Wild Bill Hickok (1837–1876) carried two .36 Navy Colts. Buffalo Bill Cody (1846–1917) is said to have preferred a Smith & Wesson.

Spur

Firing pin

Hammer (when thumbed back, it pushes spring-loaded hand against ratchet)

HOLLYWOOD HEROES
In a gunfight, no one risked shooting to wound, and only Hollywood heroes shot guns out of their opponents' hands. Gunmen never tried "fanning" (snapping the hammer back with the left hand, while holding the trigger down), because the shots might go anywhere or the hammer could stick at half-cock.

Loading gate

Spring

The gun's "hand" rotates the cylinder

Ejector

MAKING THE PEACE
The 1873 .45 Colt Peacemaker was an instant success. By 1891, the army had bought over 36,000, all with the 7.5-in (19-cm) barrel. Priced at $17, the basic model sold all over the West. Suspended in 1941, production resumed in 1955 to meet public demand.

Vulcanite (heat-hardened rubber) grip

Main spring

RESPECT FOR A GUN
Most cowboys neglected their guns and treated them with scant respect. Those whose lives depended on them, like law officers and gunfighters (pp. 42–45), took more care. Some adapted their Colts for faster firing. The lock might be filed to trip the hammer with minimum pressure, or the trigger tied back to fire by thumbing the hammer only. A fast draw was less important than a straight aim and a ruthless willingness to kill.

Butt plate, or grip

Backstrap

A FIRM GRIP
Walnut grips were factory-issue. Ivory – and even mother-of-pearl – could be supplied, though some gunmen preferred non-slip material, like deerhorn.

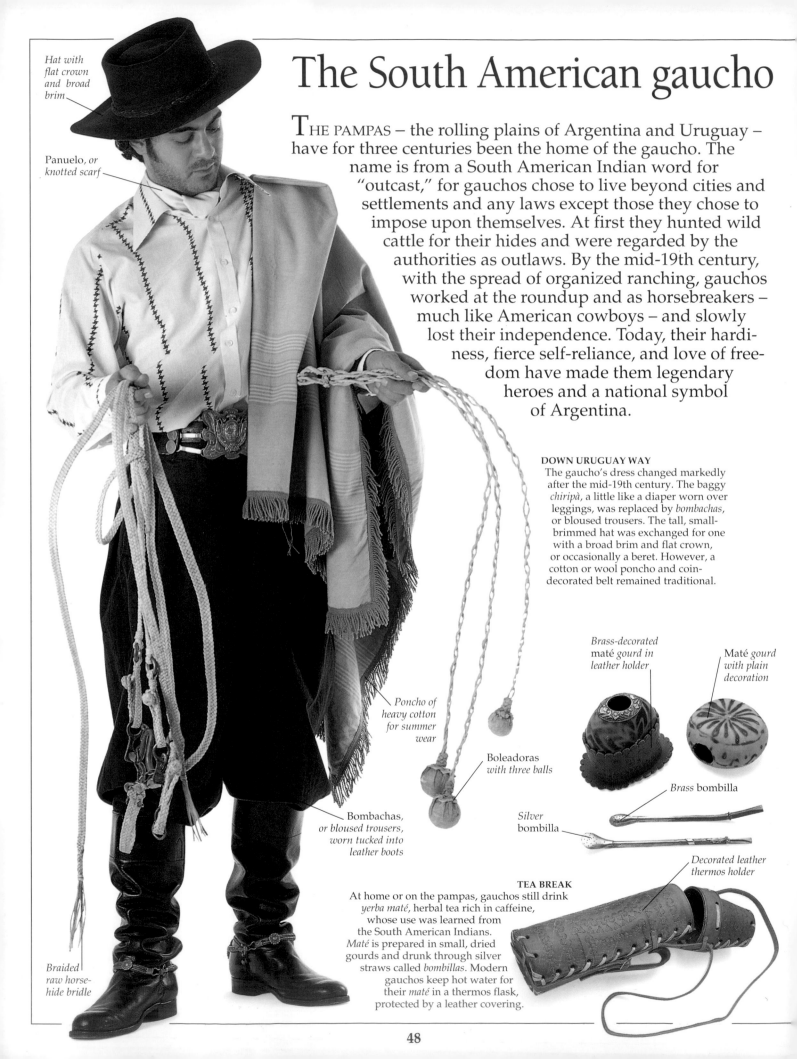

Hat with flat crown and broad brim

Panuelo, *or knotted scarf*

The South American gaucho

THE PAMPAS – the rolling plains of Argentina and Uruguay – have for three centuries been the home of the gaucho. The name is from a South American Indian word for "outcast," for gauchos chose to live beyond cities and settlements and any laws except those they chose to impose upon themselves. At first they hunted wild cattle for their hides and were regarded by the authorities as outlaws. By the mid-19th century, with the spread of organized ranching, gauchos worked at the roundup and as horsebreakers – much like American cowboys – and slowly lost their independence. Today, their hardiness, fierce self-reliance, and love of freedom have made them legendary heroes and a national symbol of Argentina.

DOWN URUGUAY WAY
The gaucho's dress changed markedly after the mid-19th century. The baggy *chiripà*, a little like a diaper worn over leggings, was replaced by *bombachas*, or bloused trousers. The tall, small-brimmed hat was exchanged for one with a broad brim and flat crown, or occasionally a beret. However, a cotton or wool poncho and coin-decorated belt remained traditional.

Brass-decorated maté *gourd in leather holder*

Maté gourd with plain decoration

Poncho of heavy cotton for summer wear

Boleadoras with three balls

Brass bombilla

Silver bombilla

Bombachas, or bloused trousers, worn tucked into leather boots

Decorated leather thermos holder

TEA BREAK
At home or on the pampas, gauchos still drink *yerba maté*, herbal tea rich in caffeine, whose use was learned from the South American Indians. *Maté* is prepared in small, dried gourds and drunk through silver straws called *bombillas*. Modern gauchos keep hot water for their *maté* in a thermos flask, protected by a leather covering.

Braided raw horse-hide bridle

Silver *facón*
contained in
a plain leather
sheath, or scabbard

Sometimes a facón
*was worn clipped
inside the boot*

20th-century pewter dress
or parade *facón* from Brazil

HUNTING AND EATING
The gaucho's *facón*, or knife, was used
for killing animals, skinning hides, and
preparing food. Worn tucked sideways into
the belt at the back, *facónes* often had silver
hafts (handles) and decorated sheaths.
In settling quarrels, gauchos despised guns
as unmanly, but knife duels were once
common up to the late 1800s.

HOMEMADE BOOTS!
Originally, gauchos rode barefoot.
Leg coverings, called *botros de potro*,
were made from the soft and pliable
leg skins of colts, many of which were
slaughtered solely for this purpose.
Angered at this loss of livestock,
ranchers from the 1850s demanded
laws against homemade "boots."

*Round stone,
covered with
raw horsehide*

Set of *boleadoras*
with three balls

DESPERATELY SEEKING RHEA
Gauchos hunted the rhea, or
South American ostrich, when
the 19th-century fashion for its
plumes made it profitable.
Using *boleadoras* with either
one or two balls, the hunters
encircled a group of birds,
then chased them individually.
To the fury of ranchers, sometimes gauchos set fire to
the pampas to scare
out the birds.

*Thong made from
braided strips of
raw horsehide*

LETHAL WEAPON –
ONE, TWO, AND THREE
The South American Indians taught the
gauchos how to use the *boleadoras*. Three
rawhide thongs, varying in length from 3–10 ft
(1–3 m), are joined at one end and at the other
tipped with metal or wooden balls or leather-
covered stones. Whirled to pick up momentum
and accurately flung at the legs, *boleadoras* will
bring down a running animal, and the entwined
thongs leave it helpless. Depending on the size
of prey, *boleadoras* with only one or two balls
are used for smaller animals and birds.

*Traditionally, coins decorated
a gaucho's belt, or* cinturon

*Elaborately engraved
silver belt buckle
added to the glamor
of a gaucho's costume*

A BAND OF SILVER
A love of silver decoration is shown in the gaucho's
broad, leather belt – the *cinturon* – often studded with
coins in addition to the heavy silver buckle. Some
gauchos wore a *faja*, or long woolen sash, instead.

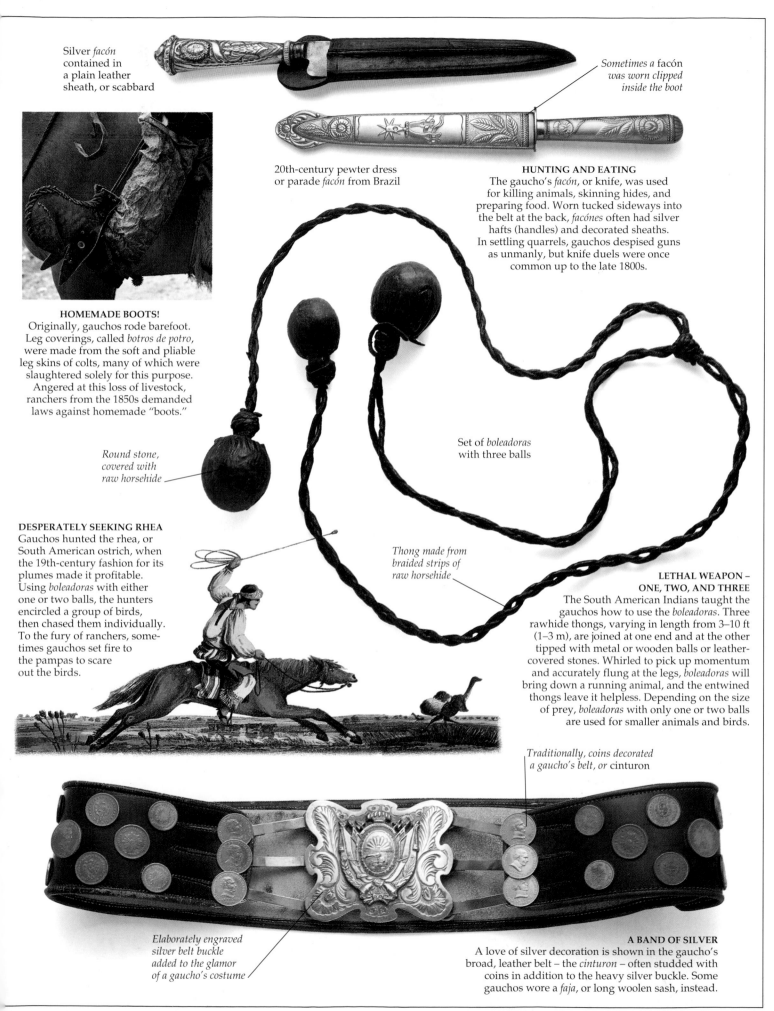

Continued on next page

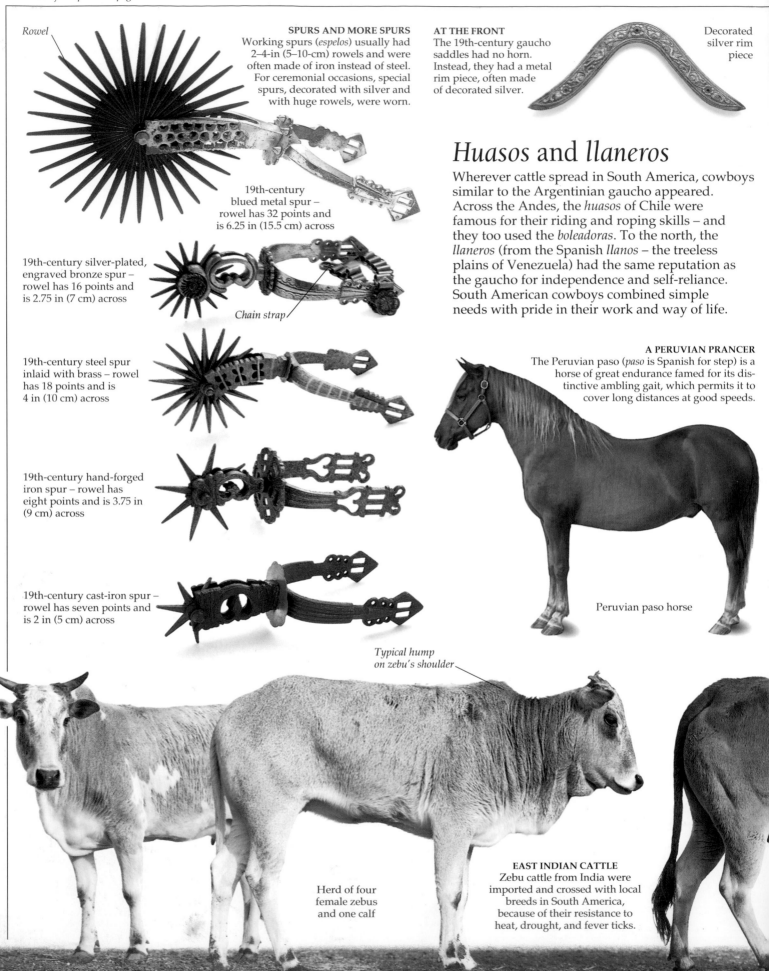

Rowel

SPURS AND MORE SPURS
Working spurs (*espelos*) usually had 2–4-in (5–10-cm) rowels and were often made of iron instead of steel. For ceremonial occasions, special spurs, decorated with silver and with huge rowels, were worn.

AT THE FRONT
The 19th-century gaucho saddles had no horn. Instead, they had a metal rim piece, often made of decorated silver.

Decorated silver rim piece

19th-century blued metal spur – rowel has 32 points and is 6.25 in (15.5 cm) across

19th-century silver-plated, engraved bronze spur – rowel has 16 points and is 2.75 in (7 cm) across

Chain strap

19th-century steel spur inlaid with brass – rowel has 18 points and is 4 in (10 cm) across

19th-century hand-forged iron spur – rowel has eight points and is 3.75 in (9 cm) across

19th-century cast-iron spur – rowel has seven points and is 2 in (5 cm) across

Huasos and llaneros

Wherever cattle spread in South America, cowboys similar to the Argentinian gaucho appeared. Across the Andes, the *huasos* of Chile were famous for their riding and roping skills – and they too used the *boleadoras*. To the north, the *llaneros* (from the Spanish *llanos* – the treeless plains of Venezuela) had the same reputation as the gaucho for independence and self-reliance. South American cowboys combined simple needs with pride in their work and way of life.

A PERUVIAN PRANCER
The Peruvian paso (*paso* is Spanish for step) is a horse of great endurance famed for its distinctive ambling gait, which permits it to cover long distances at good speeds.

Peruvian paso horse

Typical hump on zebu's shoulder

Herd of four female zebus and one calf

EAST INDIAN CATTLE
Zebu cattle from India were imported and crossed with local breeds in South America, because of their resistance to heat, drought, and fever ticks.

Very high horn

GUATEMALAN SADDLE
This modern 20th-century saddle is from Guatemala in Central America. Although this particular example was used by an English nurse who traveled on horseback to visit her patients in the countryside, it could have been used by a cowboy as a cutting saddle (pp. 32–33) because of its very high horn.

OLD-STYLE GAUCHO
Gauchos fought in Argentina's war of independence against Spain (1810–1816) and came to be seen as patriots, not outlaws. Though employed by _estancieros_ (ranchers), they needed little and tried to remain self-sufficient. This gaucho (c. 1860) from the Buenos Aires region, wears the old-style dress.

ODD-SHAPED STIRRUPS
These triangular brass stirrups (_estribos_ in Spanish) with swivel tops probably date from the 17th century. Their shape and decoration suggest they belonged to a man of position, rather than a plainsman.

Swivel top

Foliage decoration

17th-century brass stirrups

Quirt

20th-century saddle from Guatemala

Elaborate carving

BARE TOES!
Up to the mid-19th century, gauchos rode barefoot, with their big toes thrust through the stirrups. The results were alarming – foreign visitors often commented on gauchos' deformed feet.

A DIFFERENT KIND OF SLIPPER
Estancieros and other members of the upper classes could afford metal shoe stirrups for their wives and children. These offered protection and were safer, since the foot could not slip through.

Hide stirrup leather

South American stirrups were made of either metal or wood, as in this pair from Argentina

Child's brass shoe stirrup

Lady's silver shoe stirrup

IF THE STRAP FITS, WEAR IT
Poor, barefoot gauchos still wore spurs, which had to be attached to the foot by a leather heel strap. This spur seems to have been a do-it-yourself creation – the shank has been drilled in order to have a crude rowel added.

Silver keeper

Shank

South American leather heel strap, with separate rowel spur attached

Hanging fold of skin acts as radiator to get rid of excess heat

Zebu calf is 21 months old

Camargue *Gardians*

A WILD LANDSCAPE of salt marshes and sandy lagoons, the Camargue lies in the delta of the river Rhône in southern France. Hot and humid in the summer and swept by the cold *mistral* wind in winter, this part of Provence is sometimes called the "Wild West of France." *Manades*, or herds, of black fighting bulls are bred by the *manadiers* (ranchers) and tended by *gardians* (*garder* is French for "look after"), or keepers, who ride the unique white horses of the region. The *gardians* have their origins in the *gardo-besti* (cattle keepers) of the Middle Ages (A.D. 500–1350) and follow a code of honor like the chivalry and courtesy of the knights of old. The *Confrérie des Gardians* (brotherhood, or Order, of the *Gardians*) was founded in 1512. Many customs had faded until the Marquis Folco Baroncelli (1869–1943) revived them in the 1880s. He loved Provence, especially the lifestyle of the *gardians*, which he himself shared.

HERDER OF CATTLE
This *gardian* of the late 1800s is dressed in winter clothes and tends a *manade* near his *cabane*. Usually one-roomed, these cottages had the door at the south end to shelter it from the *mistral* that blows from the north.

SUNDAY BEST
The beautiful traditional women's costumes of the Arles region are worn here by wives of *gardians* of the 1920s. Originally from the reign of Louis XV (1715–1774), this traditional dress had begun to disappear until encouraged by the poet Frederic Mistral (1830–1914), leader of the movement to revive Provençal culture. Now such costumes are worn for festivals.

MODERN MOTHER AND CHILD
Today, although few of the ranch owners are women, the wives and children of *gardians* share the work with the men, tending herds of both horses and bulls. This *gardiane* wears clothes similar to the men, except for the divided riding skirt. Children help, too, and learn to ride at a very young age. This boy is wearing a waistcoat and trousers made of "moleskin" (a type of cotton). His outfit is just like his father's (right), except for the jacket.

Moleskin waistcoat

Split riding skirt

Owner's brand mark

READY FOR A PARADE
These neat spurs (right) are worn for particularly elaborate events, such as parades and festivals. They look more elegant than working spurs (below) and are less likely to startle the horse.

Parade spurs

OLD-STYLE BOOTS
These are old-style riding boots, made of leather. Nowadays, short, calf-length boots are more common, as in America. In the 1800s, some *gardians* wore *sabots*, or clogs, which had flat soles and no heels.

A pair of working spurs

A PAIR OF WORKING SPURS
Gardians wear short, steel spurs with a ten-point rowel, held on the boot by a small strap. Horses are spurred only when real speed is necessary – for example, when dodging an angry bull.

Flat-crowned, wide-brimmed black hat

Crop (nerf de boeuf) for controlling a rebellious horse

Mouscaü, or shoo fly

Typical brightly colored shirt

Trident

Black velvet jacket

Edging of decorative black ribbon

NO FLIES ON ME
The top object is a type of French quirt, used as a crop to keep young, rebellious horses under control. The *mouscaü* (bottom) was attached to the reins of the work horses and would swing from side to side to keep flies off.

Horsehair halter

Chain noseband

Leather crupper

Saddlebag containing food

Leather strap prevents horse from throwing its head back

Saddle pad

Moleskin trousers

Small rowel spur

Manadier, or ranch owner

Typical gardian saddle

Tr.oussequin, or cantle

Caban, or caped overcoat

A GARDIAN AND HIS HORSE
A modern *gardian* wears clothes that are both traditional and practical. The black velvet jacket was once common in the Mediterranean countries of Spain and Italy and was adopted by Marquis Baroncelli, who added black ribbon edging. The shirt is always brightly colored, so that if a *gardian* is thrown from his horse in the marshes he can be spotted easily by rescuers. The trousers are made of "moleskin" (a heavy cotton with a twill weave), though jeans are often worn nowadays.

OLD-STYLE GARDIAN
A *manadier* dresses in the old style for winter weather. He might be away from his *mas* (farmhouse) for several days, so the *caban* helps keep out the cold. The thigh-high boots are designed to allow him to work both in the rain and the salt marshes. In all, there are now over 80 *manadiers* who breed either Spanish or Camargais bulls.

Continued on next page

SNATCH THE RED ROSETTE

With the bull carefully secured, the red ribbon *cocarde* is centered on the bull's forehead by tying the string around the base of each horn. White tassels are also attached to each horn. Bullfighters are called *razeteurs*, from *razet* (the half circle in which they must run to grab the *cocarde*). They use a *crochet* shaped like the talons of a bird of prey. There are two types – the modern (right) and the old-style (far right).

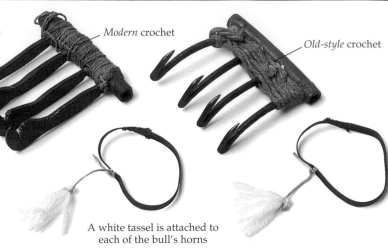

Modern crochet

Old-style crochet

A white tassel is attached to each of the bull's horns

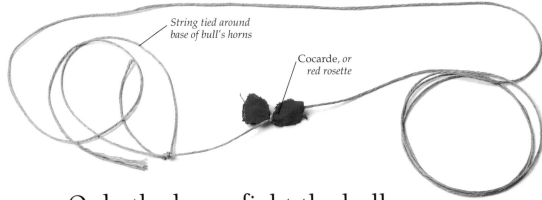

String tied around base of bull's horns

Cocarde, or red rosette

THE DRAMA OF THE BULLRING

So popular are the *courses à la cocarde*, or bullfights, that they are held in arenas. Some of these arenas date from Roman times, like this one in Arles that can hold over 23,000 people. *Courses* also take place in villages, set in improvised or permanent bullrings. *Cocardiers* are bulls that appear in the arena.

Only the brave fight the bulls

Provençal bullfights are tests of daring and skill, without the blood and death of the Spanish *corrida*. On foot, men try to snatch a *cocarde* (rosette) tied between the bull's horns, using a *crochet* (hook). A Camargue bull can charge quicker and turn more sharply than a fast horse, so the game is dangerous as well as exciting. The bulls are taken back to their *manade* (herd) when the spectacle is over. Today in the Camargue, there are around 60 breeders of the black Camargais bulls, while over 20 breed the Spanish bulls.

THE BRAVE BLACK BULL

A distinct type, the original Camargue bulls may trace their ancestry back to those of the prehistoric cave paintings at Lascaux in southern France. With black, curly, shiny coats, they are fierce and independent. Raised only for fighting, some have been crossbred with Spanish bulls since a famous *gardian*, Joseph Yonnet, began this trend in 1869.

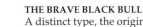

Ancient trident

Bell for leading bull or cow

BULL'S BELL

Amid the marshes of the Camargue, wandering or injured animals may be hard to find. *Gardians* tie bells around the necks of herd leaders, both cows and bulls. The bells are made of brazed sheet metal. Different sizes and shapes make different sounds, so an owner can distinguish which is his animal.

BY A NOSE

This *mouraü* is for weaning young calves. Made of willow wood, it is fitted in the calf's nose. If the calf raises its head to suckle at its mother's udder, the wood blocks its mouth, but it will swing away from the mouth if the calf lowers its head to graze.

Mouraü – for weaning young calves

ABOUT BRANDS AND BRANDING

The *ferrade* (branding) of yearlings, both horses and cattle, is a popular spectacle. Each owner has his personal mark, usually initials or a simple symbol. The brand on the right, belonging to a prominent *gardian* family, is most elaborate. The two superimposed hearts symbolize a mother and her sons. Horses also must carry the mark of the French Stud Farm Service (left) – a letter and a number indicate the year and order of birth of the foal.

Two brand marks – the left one is from the French Stud Farm Service ("E" refers to the year of birth; "5" means the fifth foal of the year); the anchor brand (right) belongs to a former sailor

Brand marks of a well-known *gardian* family – the hearts symbolize a mother (outer heart) and her two sons (the inner hearts)

ON FIRE

Camargue branding irons, which are heated in a wood fire, have longer shafts than those used in America. Bulls used to be tripped up on the run with a trident and branded as they lay on the ground. Now cattle and horses are lassoed, made to lie down, given a type of local anesthetic, and branded on the left thigh.

WILD WHITE HORSES OF THE CAMARGUE

These "white horses of the sea" have bred wild in the marshes of the Camargue for over a thousand years. They have distinctive wide heads, short necks, and long, thick manes and tails. Their very broad hooves have adapted to the soft, wet marshland. The 1951 French film *Crin Blanc* (White Mane), aroused world interest in these striking horses and the Camargue.

ANCIENT AND MODERN

The *gardian*'s trident is perhaps descended from the 14th-century knight's three-pointed jousting lance. It is still used in the fields to drive the cattle, to turn a charging bull, or to separate the bulls, which will fight to the death sometimes. In the arena, there used to be a contest where a bull's repeated charges would be stopped by two men with tridents.

The *gardian*'s flag, made of gold embroidery on red silk, depicts St. George and the dragon

Modern trident

ST. GEORGE AND THE DRAGON

The *Confrérie des Gardians* had only 37 members at the beginning of the 16th century, but now has 350. Under the leadership of an annually elected *capitaine*, the society (which has its festival on April 23 every year) undertakes charity and welfare work for the widows and families of *gardians*. The standard, or flag, of the *Confrérie* dates from the 1820s. Made of crimson embroidered silk, it carries the emblem of St. George slaying the dragon.

Cowboys down under

Oɴ ᴛʜᴇ ᴅʀɪᴇsᴛ ᴏғ ᴀʟʟ ᴛʜᴇ ᴄᴏɴᴛɪɴᴇɴᴛs, raising cattle in Australia's vast outback has never been easy, though it has been an important industry since the 1830s. The stockman, or "ringer" – from ringing, or circling, the mob (herd) at night – has become a legend like the American cowboy. For mustering (rounding up) and droving he rode a waler, a distinctive breed from New South Wales. However, the legend belies the fact that many stockmen were Aborigines or, indeed, women. And today, jackeroos (trainee cattle station managers) have been joined by jilleroos. Stations can be huge – some average over 500,000 acres (200,000 hectares). Light airplanes, helicopters, and motorcycles are replacing horses for mustering. Australia now has more cattle (24 million) than people (17 million). By eating the land bare during drought, cattle are becoming a threat to the environment.

ABORIGINAL STOCKMEN
Australia's original inhabitants (the Aborigines) were made to work on outback cattle stations in the 1800s. However, Aborigines quickly adapted to stock work and made it part of their way of life. Since the 1970s they have been buying and running their own cattle stations.

CRACKING THE WHIP
Drovers carried guns only to shoot older bulls in unmustered country in order to gain control of the mob. The drover's 6–7-ft (1.8–2.1-m) long stockwhip was his main work tool. Made from intricately braided leather, it cracks like a pistol shot.

Finely braided kangaroo hide

Stockwhip, c. 1890s

Tin for holding matches

Knife

Watch

Stockman's belt

Quart pot

Water bags

SURVIVAL KIT
From the Kimberley area of Western Australia, this handmade leather belt holds a stockman's knife, a tin for matches, and a watch. The quart pot (holding 2 pints) is for boiling water. The water bags hold 2 pints (1.1 liters) each – one for drinking and the other for cooking.

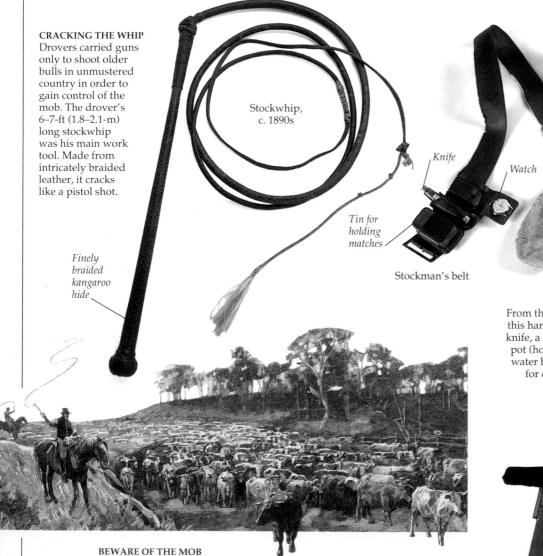

BEWARE OF THE MOB
Stockmen drove mobs of cattle incredible distances across the continent (pp. 38–39). Nat Buchanan pioneered stock routes from Queensland into the Northern Territory. In 1883, he and 70 drovers brought 20,000 shorthorns 1,800 miles (3,000 km) to stock Victoria River Downs.

INTO THE FAR COUNTRY
For mustering and droving trips, pack saddles carried food and essential equipment. They were expected to endure long, hard use, so were made from and repaired with greenhide (untanned leather).

Pack saddle made from greenhide

Leather band on felt akubra hat

Wide wings were common on Australian saddles (but never a horn)

Metal stirrups typical of stockman's saddle

Split at back of coat eases movement while riding a horse

Braided rawhide quirt

Drizabone coat made from oiled sailcloth

Australian stockman with typical gear

Back view of stockman

AN AUSTRALIAN LEGEND
The legendary bushranger (bandit) Ned Kelly (1855–1880) came from the Australian-Irish community, persecuted in the mid-1800s by land laws and the police. He was a horse and cattle thief, then a bank robber. Finally, despite his iron helmet and body armor, he was captured and hanged.

THE AUSTRALIAN STOCKMAN
This stockman is dressed for the wet weather season. The Drizabone coat is a direct descendant of those made from oiled sailcloth of the 1800s. Jeans are an alternative to "moleskin" (heavy cotton twill) trousers. His akubra hat (pp. 20–21) is curled at the edge to prevent the brim from buckling. Unlike American cowboys, his boots (pp. 24–25) are only ankle high and his saddle (pp. 14–15) has no horn.

MODERN MUSTERING
Modern mustering is still hard work but has become more mechanized. A wagonette brings food, and many drovers ride motorcycles. Dogs are still valued, however, especially the famous blue heeler. Bred from several dog strains, including the dingo, they nip the heels of cattle!

Cowgirls

ON THE WORLD'S CATTLE FRONTIERS in the 1800s, women made their own contribution to taming the wilderness. Those who married worked desperately hard to make homes in grim conditions – and many died of it. In the American West, cowgirls as such were unknown until recent times, though there were some cattle baronesses, like Susan McSween, widow of one of the participants killed in the Lincoln County War (pp. 44–45) in 1878. Hollywood has glamorized the job of saloon girl, at best a brief and unrewarding career. Some women turned to crime and had their exploits exaggerated by a sensationalist press, like those of "Cattle Annie" McDougal and Jennie "Little Britches" Stevens in 1893–1894.

"WHEN THEY WERE BAD, THEY WERE HORRID"
Belle Starr (1848–1889), the "Bandit Queen," was invented by newspapers and dime novelists. The real Belle had a procession of outlaw boyfriends, then organized her own small-time gang in Indian territory, until she was shot – possibly by her own son.

AUSTRALIA'S JILLEROOS
Jackeroos, those who aimed to become managers of Australia's cattle stations, have traditionally learned the business by first working as stockmen (pp. 56–57). In recent years, so too have more and more women, like these two jilleroos from New South Wales.

CANADIAN COWGIRL
Wives and daughters of Canadian ranchers came to share range work as strict 19th-century attitudes toward women faded. This camera-shy cowgirl (c. 1920) from western Canada wears a cowboy's outfit, including the uneasy addition of a pistol.

1 FAST LADY
Once freed from social rules that denied them the opportunity, women were able to prove that they could ride as fast and as skillfully as men – for example, in the demonstration of range skills in the rodeo (pp. 62–63).

Light touch of rein to neck guides horse around barrel

2 TOUGH COMPETITION
In the U.S., Canada, and Australia, the regular women's event in most rodeos is barrel racing, which is based on the technique of cutting out cows from the herd. Each rider races her horse in a cloverleaf pattern around three empty oil drums, placed in a triangle. The fastest time wins, but 5 seconds is added for every barrel knocked over.

Body leans in direction that rider wants horse to take

CALAMITY JANE
Martha "Calamity Jane" Cannary (1852?–1903) became famous for wearing men's clothes, swearing, and drinking. She hung around army and mining camps but, despite the legend, was never a scout nor a girlfriend of Wild Bill Hickok (pp. 42–43). Dime novelists made her a pistol-packing terror, and she tried to trade on that image.

Poster advertising the amazing feats of marksmanship exhibited by Annie Oakley in Buffalo Bill's Wild West show

"LITTLE SURE SHOT"
Phoebe "Annie Oakley" Moses (1860–1926), the incredible trick-shot star of Buffalo Bill Cody's Wild West show (pp. 60–61), is remembered as a western superwoman. In fact, born in Ohio, she visited the West only with the show. However, her legend was immortalized on stage and screen by the hit musical *Annie Get Your Gun*.

3 PEAK FITNESS
If the horse has to be particularly agile and in top condition to compete in barrel racing, the rider, too, must be fit. Great skill and confidence are needed for this event.

Rider's feet must be kept close to sides of horse to avoid knocking the barrel over

Split skirt

Flank muscles are well-developed to help achieve high speeds

4 WOMEN ONLY
All-girl rodeos are popular. Like cowboys, cowgirls compete in bareback bronc-riding, tie-down calf roping, goat tying, and snatching a ribbon from a running steer's back. All these events have to be performed at extreme speed.

KEEPING UP THE TRADITION
The wives and daughters of the *gardians* of the Camargue in southern France (pp. 52–55) are as much involved in the work of tending the herds of unique horses and bulls as the men. Women wear the same mixture of traditional and practical dress as the men – except for a divided riding skirt!

Cowboy culture

An advertisement for guns depicts the cowboy myth

THE COWBOY HAS RIDDEN OFF THE RANGE of reality into a new life as a mythical hero. This strange process was well under way by 1900; surviving "saddle tramps" from the Old West must have been surprised. Wild West shows of the 1880s starred cowboys as dashing men of action. Then writers created the strong, silent cowboy, slow to act but invincible when angered. From 1903, the new film industry snapped up this ready-made hero and guaranteed his popularity. So powerful is the cowboy's romantic image that it has found expression in music and fashion and has been used eagerly by advertisers. Fantasies about the man with his horse and gun, riding the wide open spaces, are a theme of the 20th century.

DUDE COWBOYS
Carrying cameras instead of guns, the dude cowboys of today try to recreate the excitement of the West without having to undergo the severe hardships endured by the true cowboy.

FROM GUNS TO GUITARS
"Cowboy" singers became popular on radio in the 1920s and in sound films after 1928. Most famous was Gene Autry (b. 1907) who, riding "Champion the Wonder Horse" in 95 movies, showed a cowboy pure in thought and deed. Guitar-strumming Roy Rogers (b. 1912), the top western star from 1942 to 1954, also rode a famous horse: "Trigger." Audiences, mostly young, eventually saw that a cowboy's guitar was as important as his gun. Both stars had their own TV series in 1950–1951.

THE FIRST WESTERN SUPERSTAR
Tom Mix (1880–1940) made nearly 300 films and was the first western superstar. He deliberately mixed furious action with flamboyant dress to give the cowboy a spectacular image.

Tom Mix's hat, specially designed for him by the Stetson company

Tom Mix's gun

THE RISE OF THE MYTH
Hollywood has made more westerns than any other kind of film. Early silent stars like William S. Hart (1865–1946) began a trend later firmly followed by John Wayne (1907–1979) – the cowboy hero as a rugged individualist doing right at the point of a gun. Since the mid-1960s, Clint Eastwood (b. 1930) has portrayed a grimmer hero in a grittier West.

THE SHOWMAN OF THE WEST

Buffalo Bill Cody (1846–1917) began the first Wild West show in 1883. He made cowboys the main attraction and created the first cowboy star – William "Buck" Taylor (1857–1924). The show toured America and Europe until 1916 to audiences totaling millions. Cody was a superb showman, and his cowboys performed feats of skill, daring, and drama. This was the image forever fixed in the public's mind.

Bronze bust of Buffalo Bill Cody

Stetson worn – even when entertaining

Shoestring tie with decorative silver heart

Fringing originally worn to encourage rain to fall from clothes – not as sometimes thought – to keep off flies

COUNTRY HOEDOWN

A typical western style of dancing is called square dancing, where four couples form a square. "Swing your partner," "do-si-do," and other instructions are shouted out by a "caller."

SLAVE TO FASHION

Advertisers in the 1950s and 1960s kept stressing that cowboys had a good time. A fad for western fashion in the late 1970s and 1980s followed, but the image was of leisure, not hard work.

Gun belt belonging to western writer Earle Forrest

THE PEN IS MIGHTIER ... THAN THE GUN

Western writers were the real inventors of the cowboy hero. Owen Wister (1860–1938) had a huge success with *The Virginian* in 1902. Soon he was followed by Zane Grey (1872–1939) who wrote 78 novels, and Max Brand (1892–1944) who churned out over 300. Hollywood made films of many of these stories. Most bore no relation to reality, despite some writers, like Earle Forrest (above), who actually worked in the West.

Rodeo thrills and spills

COWBOYS' SKILLS ARE SPECTACULAR – how natural that they should be turned into a paying spectacle. Rodeos (from the Spanish for roundup) probably began as friendly competitions between cowboys when trail herds met. From the 1880s on, they became formal events and were later professionalized in the 1930s. Since 1945, the Rodeo Cowboys Association has controlled what is one of the biggest spectator sports in the U.S., with over 500 rodeos annually. In Canada, the famous Calgary Stampede began in 1912, and the Australian Rough Riders Association organizes big prize meetings. The five traditional rodeo events are saddle bronc riding, calf roping, bareback bronc riding, steer wrestling, and brahman bull riding. The first two are range skills, but the last three also show strength and daring. The Calgary Stampede has added chuck wagon racing. Rodeo is now show business – part contest and part circus – and U.S. rodeos offer over $15 million in prize money each year.

1 CALF ROPING
Calf roping requires both cooperation between horse and rider and skill with a lariat (pp. 34–35). The cowboy chases a calf and ropes it (he is disqualified if he misses), ties the rope to the saddlehorn, and leaps from his horse.

AROUND AND AROUND
Barrel racing requires some of the same skills as cutting out a calf from the herd (pp. 32–33). It is the traditional cowgirls' event in rodeo (pp. 58–59).

RIDE 'EM COWBOY!
In saddle bronc riding, the cowboy uses a hornless saddle and a single rein attached to a halter – as depicted in this painting *Bucked: A Rodeo Thrill* by Stanley L. Wood (1866–1928). The cowboy mounts the horse in a chute (enclosure); on its release he must hold the rein in one hand, keeping the other free, spur the horse, and stay on for eight seconds. Points are earned by the rider for style – and by the horse for bucking properly! In any case, it is not a pleasant experience for the horse – or the rider either, particularly if he falls off.

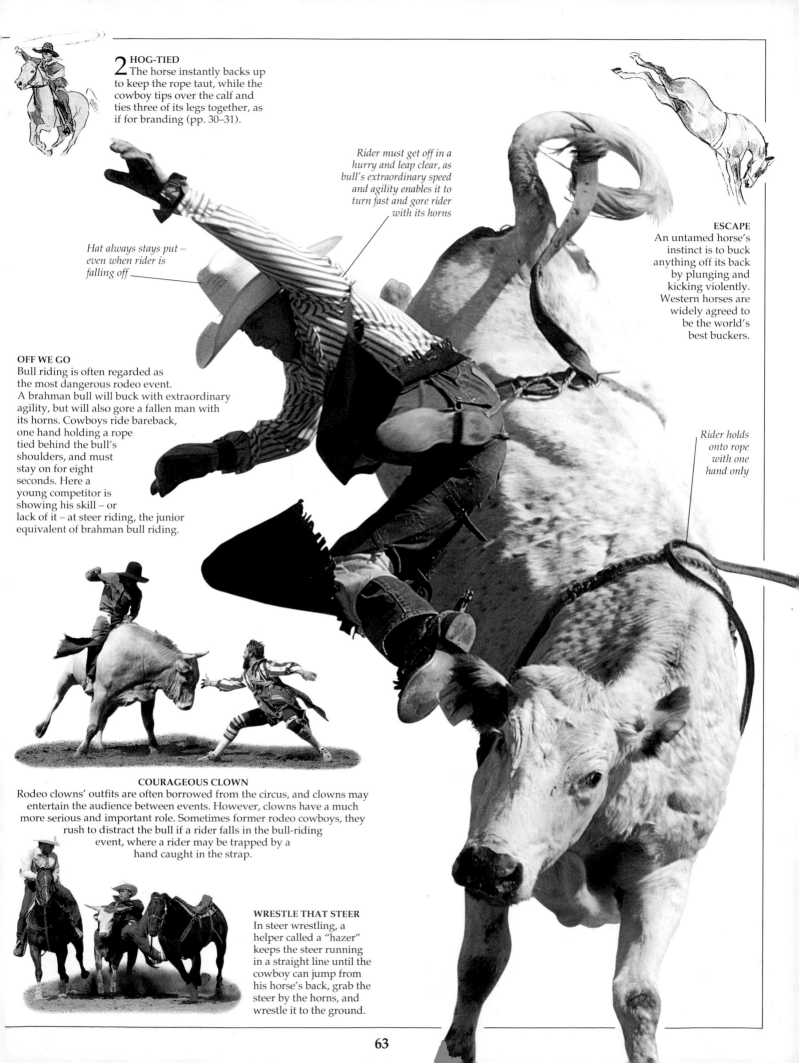

2 HOG-TIED
The horse instantly backs up to keep the rope taut, while the cowboy tips over the calf and ties three of its legs together, as if for branding (pp. 30–31).

Rider must get off in a hurry and leap clear, as bull's extraordinary speed and agility enables it to turn fast and gore rider with its horns

Hat always stays put – even when rider is falling off

ESCAPE
An untamed horse's instinct is to buck anything off its back by plunging and kicking violently. Western horses are widely agreed to be the world's best buckers.

OFF WE GO
Bull riding is often regarded as the most dangerous rodeo event. A brahman bull will buck with extraordinary agility, but will also gore a fallen man with its horns. Cowboys ride bareback, one hand holding a rope tied behind the bull's shoulders, and must stay on for eight seconds. Here a young competitor is showing his skill – or lack of it – at steer riding, the junior equivalent of brahman bull riding.

Rider holds onto rope with one hand only

COURAGEOUS CLOWN
Rodeo clowns' outfits are often borrowed from the circus, and clowns may entertain the audience between events. However, clowns have a much more serious and important role. Sometimes former rodeo cowboys, they rush to distract the bull if a rider falls in the bull-riding event, where a rider may be trapped by a hand caught in the strap.

WRESTLE THAT STEER
In steer wrestling, a helper called a "hazer" keeps the steer running in a straight line until the cowboy can jump from his horse's back, grab the steer by the horns, and wrestle it to the ground.

Index

A

Aborigines 38, 56
African-Americans 18
Allen & Wheelock gun 44
Annie Oakley 59
Australian Rough Riders
Association 62
Autry, Gene 60

B

barbed wire 28
Baroncelli, Marquis 52–53
barrel racing 58–59, 62
bears 40
bedroll 17, 22, 36–37, 41
bell (lead animals) 13, 54
belt buckles 23, 49, 61
Billy the Kid 45
bits 16–17; marmaluke 16
blue heeler 57
Bohlin, Edward H. 9, 15
boleadoras 48–49
bombachas 48
bombilla 48
boots 22–27, 41, 49, 52–53,
57; *botros de potro* 49
bosal 26
Bowie, Colonel James 38
Brand, Max 61
brands/branding 19, 24,
26, 30–32, 34, 52, 55, 63
breaking horses 11–12,
19, 48
bridles 9–10, 12, 16–17,
27, 48, 53; hackamore
12, 16; headstall 16, 26
bronc riding: bareback 59,
62; saddle 62
Buchanan, Nat 56
bucking horses 62–63
buffalo 30, 40, 45
bullfighting 13, 54
bull riding 62–63
bulls 6, 30–31, 52–55
buttero 6

C

caban 53
cabane 28, 52–53

Calamity Jane 59
calf roping 34, 59, 62–63
Calgary Stampede 62
Carson, Kit 47
cattle 6–8, 30–35, 38–41,
48; Aberdeen angus
30–31, 33; Hereford
30–31, 33; longhorn 8,
25, 28, 30, 38, 41; shorthorn 30–31, 56; zebu
33, 50–51, 63
"Cattle Annie" 58
cattle station 28–29, 56, 58
cattle trails 24, 36, 38–39,
42; dangers 40–41
chaparejos (chaps): *armitas*
24, 26–27; batwing 7,
18–19, 26–27; shotgun
23, 26; woolies 19, 26
chap hook 24–25
charros 7–11
Chisholm, Jesse 39
chuck wagon 36–37;
racing 62
cinch (girth) 10–12, 14–17,
35
cinturon 49
Clantons 43
clothes: American cow-
boy 7, 16–19, 22–23,
26–27, 39, 41; *charro*
7–9; *gardian* 6, 52–53;
gaucho 48–49; stock-
man 37; *vaquero* 11
cocarde/cocardiers 54
Cody, Buffalo Bill 11, 47,
61; Wild West shows
11, 14, 34, 59–61
Colt guns/rifles 8, 22,
26–27, 40, 44–47
Colt, Samuel 47
conchas 7–9, 11, 15, 24–27
Confrérie des Gardians 52
Cortés, Hernando 9
course à la cocarde 31, 54
cowgirls 32–33, 58–59,
61–62
cow towns 42
crochet 54
csikosok 7
cuffs 22, 26
cutting cattle 32–35
"cutting critter" 33

D E

dally 35
Dalton, Emmett 45
"Deadwood Dick" 18
Desperate Dan 36

drag rider 40
drovers 18, 56–57
dude cowboys 60
Earp, Virgil 42; Wyatt 43
Eastwood, Clint 60
espelos 50
estancieros 51
estribos 51

F G

facón 49
ferrade 31, 55
Forrest, Earle 61
Garcia, G. S. 11
gardians/gardianes 6, 14,
20, 28, 52–55, 59
Garrett, Pat 45
gauchos 6, 10, 12, 29,
48–51
goat tying 59
Goodnight, Charles 37, 39
Grey, Zane 61
guardia rurales 43
guns 8, 22–23, 26–27, 40,
44–47, 60
gunslingers 42–45, 47

H

hacendado 8
hacienda 9
Hardin, John Wesley 45
Hart, William S. 60
hats 18–21, 23, 26–27, 48,
53, 57, 60; akubra 20,
57; sombreros 9, 11,
20–21; ten gallon 21
Hickok, Wild Bill 42–43,
47, 59
hobbles 17
holster 8, 22–23, 27
honda 34
horses 12–13, 32–35;
American saddlebred
8–9; Andalusian 6–8,
12–13; appaloosa 19;
barb 6; Camargue 6,
13, 52–53, 55; criollo
8, 11–12; Don 13; lusi-
tano 13; maremmana
6; mustang 6–8, 12, 32;
nonius 13; Peruvian
paso 8, 50; pinto 19;
Przewalski 12; quarter
horse 13, 17, 19, 32;
thoroughbred 12;
waler 56
huaso 6, 50

I J K

Indian Police 43
jackeroos/jilleroos 56, 58
James family 42; Frank
44; Jesse 44
Kamehameha III, King 10
Kelly, Ned 57
knives 38, 49; bowie 38

L

Lake, Stuart 43
lariat 12–13, 17, 22, 26–27,
34–35
law badges 42–43
lawmen 42–45, 47
line camp 28
"Little Britches" 58
llanero 6, 50
long johns 22
Love, Nat 18
Lozano, David 8
Lucky Luke 21

M

mail order catalog 22, 29
manades/manadiers 52–53
mas 53
Masterson, Bat 43
mavericks 31
McSween, Susan 58
Meager, Michael 42
meatpackers 31
mecate 26
Mistral, Frederic 52
Mix, Tom 21, 24, 60
mob (of cattle) 56
Mongolian herdsmen 29,
35; Kazakh 12
"Morris" 21
mouraü 54
mouscaü 53
"mule ears" 24–25
mustering 56–57

N O P

Native Americans 7–8,
12, 19, 40–42, 48–49;
Nez Percé tribe 19
nerf de boeuf 53
Newton, Thomas 9
Nix, Evett 43
O.K. Corral 43

paniolo 10
panuelo 48
"piggin' string" 34
Pinkertons 42
polling 31
pony: Argentinian polo
12; Mongol 12; Texas
cow 12, 17

Q R

quirt (whip) 11–12, 15, 17,
20, 27, 51, 53, 57
railroads 38–39
ranch 28–29
ranchos 29
razeteurs 54
reining patterns 32
reins 16–17, 26, 32–33
Remington, Frederic 12,
19, 26, 42, 44
Remington guns 27, 45
rifles 26, 36, 40, 45–46
rodeo 18, 23–25, 34–35,
58–59, 62–63; clowns
63
Rodeo Cowboys
Association 62
Rogers, Roy 20, 60
Rogers, Will 34
romals 17
Roosevelt, Theodore 19
ropes and roping 24, 32,
34–35, 50
roundup 32, 48; modern
19
Russell, Charles 26
rustlers 31

S T

sabots 52
saddlebags 8, 13, 17, 53
saddle blanket 9, 17, 23
saddlemaking 8–9, 16
saddles 7–10, 14–18, 23,
35, 50–51, 53, 56–57
saddling a horse 16–17
seden 14
Sharps rifle 45
shoo fly 11, 53
sidesaddle, ladies 8
Simpson, Charles 35
Smith & Wesson gun 44,
60
Spanish conquistadors
7–9, 13, 16, 24, 30, 38
spurs: gal-leg 24; jinglebob 11, 24–25; prick 11,
24; rowel, 11, 23–27,
50–53; shank 11, 25
square dancing 61
stampede, cattle 40
Starr, Belle 58
Starr revolver 40
steer wrestling 62–63
Stetson, J.B. 21; label 20
stirrups 8, 16, 23, 51, 57;
shoe 8, 51
stockmen 20, 56–58
stock routes 38, 56
stockwhip 56

T

talabarteria 8
tapaderos (taps) 8, 14–15,
23
Taylor, "Buck" 61
Texas 18–19, 23–24, 27,
29, 30, 38–39, 45
Texas Rangers 42, 47
Thomas, Heck 43
tobacco, Bull Durham 36
trail drives 18, 38–41
trident 53–55
troussequin 53
Twain, Mark 43

V W Y

vaquero 7–11, 21, 26, 31,
33–34
Walker, Captain Samuel
46
watches, pocket 22, 56
water containers 41;
supply 28, 40–41, 56
Watkins, Dudley D. 36
Wayne, John 26, 60
Wells, Fargo 42, 44
Western advertisements,
fashion, films, books,
magazines, music 6, 9,
18, 20–21, 24, 31–32, 43,
47, 55, 60–61
Wheeler, Edward L. 18
"wild rag" 26
Winchester rifle 45–46
windmill 29
Wister, Owen 61
wolf 40
Wood, Stanley L. 41, 62
Yonnet, Joseph 54
Yosemite Sam 45
yurt 29

Acknowledgments

Dorling Kindersley would like to thank:
The Mailhan family (Marcel, Pascal, Caroline, Raoul, and Jacques), Roger and Louis Galeron, and Mme. Françoise Yonnet for providing props, animals, and models for the photo shoot in the Camargue, and Céline Carez for organizing the trip. Graham and Karen Aston, BAPTY & Company Ltd, The Rev. Peter Birkett MA, Brian Borrer's Artistry in Leather (Western Saddlemaker), Goodey's Foxhill Stables & Carriage Repository, J.D. Consultancy (agent for J. B. Collection), Bryan Mickleburgh's American Costumes & Props, Ros Pearson's Avon Western Wear, David Gainsborough Roberts, and Walsall Leather Museum for providing props for photography.

Pam and Paul Brown of Zara Stud, Peter and Mandy Richman of Cotmarsh Horned Pedigree Hereford/Creeslea Aberdeen Angus (Swindon), Sterling Quarter Horses, Val Taylor's Moores Farm, Twycross Zoo, and Sheila Whelan's The Avenue Riding Centre for providing animals and riding arenas for photography.
Karl Bandy, The Rev. Peter Birkett, Brian Borrer, Pam and Paul Brown, John Denslow, Wayne Findlay, Dave Morgan, Andrew Nash, Helen Parker, Scott Steedman, Francesca Sternberg, and J.B. Warriner as models.
Bob Gordon, Manisha Patel, Sharon Spencer, Helena Spiteri, and Scott Steedman for editorial/design help.
Lucky Productions S.A., Geneva, Switzerland for permission to reproduce "Lucky Luke".

Authenticators: Graham Aston, Jane Lake, and James White
Index: Lynne Bresler
Map: Sallie Alane Reason
Model: Gordon Models
Mongolian paintings: Ts Davaahuu

Picture credits
a=above, b=below, c=center, l=left, r=right
Australian Picture Library, Sydney 58cl.
Australian Stockman's Hall of Fame 56cr, 56br.
Bettmann Archive, New York 40tr.
Bruce Coleman 36ct, 36cl, 36cb.
Culver Pictures Inc., New York 39bc.
© Dorling Kindersley: Bob Langrish 6–7ct, 13tr, 13ctr, 13cbr, 13cb, 18–19ct, 19c, 19cr, 50cr; Jerry Young 40bl, 40br, 41cl, 41c; Dave King 45t, 47cr.
Mary Evans Picture Library 6tl, 7cr, 7br, 13br, 25br, 31cr, 33cr, 34tl, 51tr, 56bl, 57tr.
Ronald Grant Archive 45bc.

Hamlyn Publishing Group (from *The Book of the West* by Charles Chilton, © Charles Chilton 1961) 60tl.
Guy Hetherington & Mary Plant 29tr, 35t.
Hulton Deutsche/Bettmann Archive 45br.
Hutchinson Library 6cl, 12cl, 49tl.
Kobal Collection 21tr, 60l.
Bob Langrish 10bl 10bc, 11tl, 12bl, 32tl, 33tl, 33tc, 33tr, 34bl, 34cr, 58bl, 58br, 59cl, 59b, 59br, 62l, 63cl, 63bl, 63r.
From the "Dalton Brothers Memory Game" published with the authorization of LUCKY PRODUCTIONS S.A., GENEVA, SWITZERLAND 21br.
Peter Newark's Western Americana and Historical Pictures 11cbr, 12tl, 17bl, 18bl, 19bc, 20tr, 26bl, 28tl, 30cl, 31br, 37br, 38tl, 39bl, 41tl, 41bl, 42cr, 43cl, 45ct, 47tc, 58tl, 58tr, 59tl, 59tc, 59tr, 60tr, 60cb, 60br, 63cr.
Photographic Library of Australia, Sydney: Robin Smith 29cl, 56tl; Richard Holdendorp 57br.
© D.C. Thompson & Co. Ltd. 36bl.

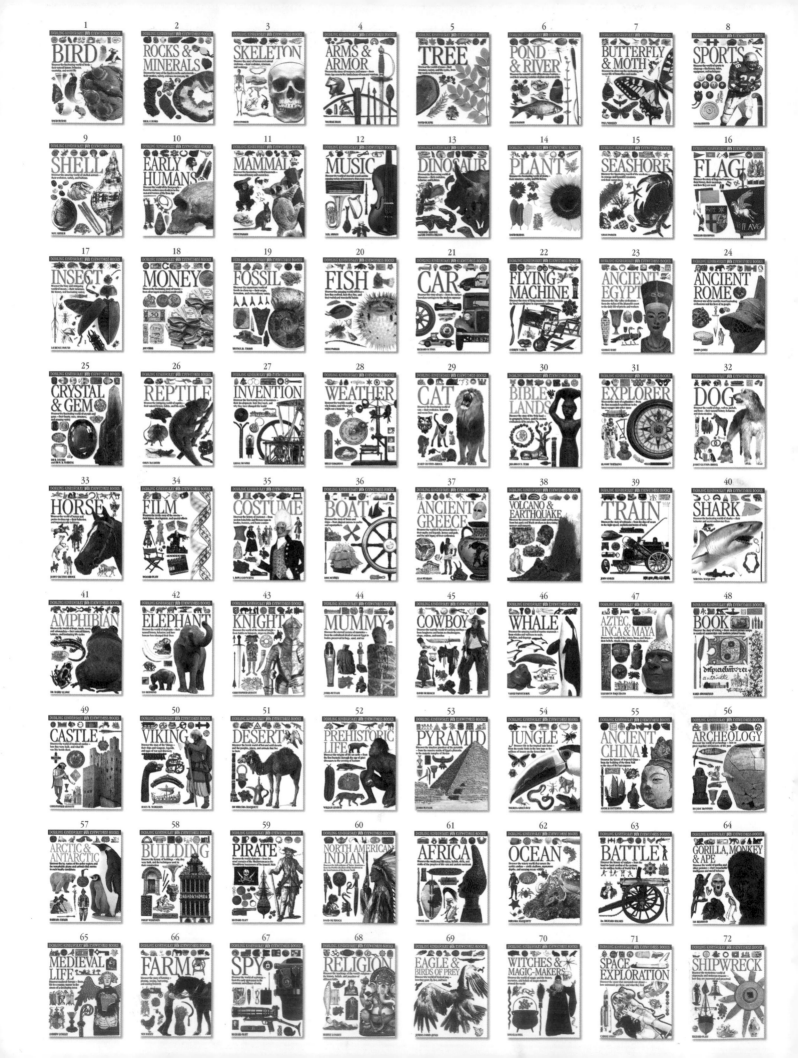